crafts for kids

crafts for kids

Gill Dickinson

hamlyn

introduction 6

mother's day
father's day,
valentine's day
8

easter
24

halloween
40

thanksgiving &
harvest festival
58

First published in Great Britain in 2003

by Hamlyn, a division of Octopus Publishing Ltd, 2–4 Heron Quays, London E14 4JP

Copyright © Octopus Publishing Group Ltd 2003

The right of Gill Dickinson to be identified as the author of this work has been asserted by her in accordance with the Copyright, Designs and Patents Act, 1988.

Distributed in the United States and Canada by Sterling Publishing Co., Inc. 387 Park Avenue South, New York, NY 10016-8810

ISBN 0 600 60692 9

A CIP catalogue record for this book is available from the British Library.

Printed and bound in China

10 9 8 7 6 5 4 3 2 1

Disclaimer
The publishers cannot accept any legal responsibility or liability for accidents or damage arising from the use of any items mentioned in this book or in the carrying out of any of the projects.

contents

introduction

Festive occasions take place all around the world every day of the year. People like to join together to celebrate personal events such as birthdays and anniversaries and they enjoy communal cultural or religious festivals such as Halloween and Christmas, too. Children in particular love to participate – whatever the occasion – whether it's making a monster mask for Halloween that they can look forward to wearing, or sticking down brightly coloured paper to make a birthday card for a brother or sister. The simple projects in this book should be inspirational and fun to make for one of these special events.

creative ideas for kids

Being able to create something special is important for everyone, but particularly so for children. They can start from a really young age, first by observing parents or siblings and gradually participating more and more until they have the satisfaction of producing something all by themselves. To choose the colours and materials that they like should be a rewarding and satisfying part of the experience.

Apart from having fun creating a mask, finger puppet or birthday card, it is good for children to make things for other people, so they can enjoy giving to someone else. A handmade item is so much more special than something bought ready made and will be much appreciated, especially by doting parents and grandparents.

about this book

Each chapter includes a variety of themed projects with easy-to-follow step-by-step instructions as well as suggested variations. A range of templates is given at the back of the book. Safety is a key issue, so adult supervision and assistance is always advisable, especially when cooking and using knives, scissors and dyes. It also helps to control the mess! The making times and age ranges are given as a loose guide, but be led by your child, and remember that most children will derive satisfaction from even the tiniest contribution.

materials

The range of craft materials available is vast and exciting, and although you may wish to buy some specialist items, you can keep the budget low by using what you have around the house. Recycle items such as newspapers, tin cans, yoghurt pots and cardboard tubes, and keep a box of scraps: papers, ribbons, wool, buttons and other unwanted bits and pieces. Children can be innovative at very little cost, making papier-mâché shapes from newspaper, water and PVA glue, painting plastic pots with brightly coloured paints or making a pretty decorated tree from an old cardboard tube. When buying any equipment or materials, always check it is safe for children and non-toxic.

paper

Most craft projects will require you to use paper at some point. Fortunately, it is versatile and strong. Coloured tissue, crêpe, patterned, tracing and parcel papers are usually available at most art and craft shops. Papers can be cut, punched, folded, torn, scrunched-up or even used as a stencil. Always have a selection handy and keep any scraps that are left over.

paints and pens

Poster paints are good and adequate for most projects. For special effects such as papier-mâché jewellery, there are fluorescent acrylics. These give a luminous quality, cover well and can be used time and time again. Decorating with fabric dyes, paints and felt-tipped pens is fun but can be messy. Glow-in-the-dark and 3-D puff paints are perfect for the Halloween costumes, not to mention other projects. Felt-tipped pens, coloured wax and chalk crayons are always a good standby and can be used in conjunction with other materials.

glues

PVA glue is non-toxic, very strong and can be used for most projects. Always use stick glue on tissue and crêpe paper as water-based glues (such as PVA) and paints dissolve them. Glitter glues are usually non-toxic and they come in amazing colours from primary and metallic to iridescent greens and blues. These glues are simple and safe to use and look stunning when dry. If a project is looking a little dull, jazz it up with a touch of glitter glue and you will be surprised at the result.

pipe cleaners

Coloured chenilles and pipe cleaners are essential for the craft box: they can be bent, curled, cut, and used by young and old alike. They are useful for a wide range of ideas, tied round a gift instead of a ribbon, threaded with beads for a necklace or used for a three-dimensional card. Whatever their use, they come in a vast range of colours and widths and are fun and pleasurable to work with.

specialist craft items

Look out for decorative punches and scissors; these are easy to use and many are especially designed for younger children. Pre-cut foam shapes, self-stick notes and bags of mixed gummed paper shapes are brilliant for children to use. They get instant results and feel they are participating with older members of the family by decorating a birthday card, making paper bunting or a piece of jewellery. Although not as creative as using other materials, ready-made items are bright and appealing and can be made into something quickly, which can be beneficial especially when very small children or those lacking in confidence are involved.

all that glitters

Coloured glitters, beads and sequins can be added as a finishing touch to many projects. None of these tiny glittery items should ever be left in the hands of very young children but used only in the presence of an adult.

A child's imagination should be stimulated by creating and making things. Help your children to tackle these festive projects and you'll have hours of entertainment.

go on, enjoy yourselves!

mother's day,
father's day,
valentine's day

T-shirt card

ages 5–6 years

This card and the variations all resemble clothing and are folded in half so they stand up. They offer a great opportunity to gather scraps of fabric, buttons, braid and lace to make an original card that will be worth having as a keepsake.

1 Make sure the white paper is large enough for your card. Cut a piece of fabric to exactly the same size as the paper. Glue the fabric smoothly, right side up, onto the card.

2 Draw a T-shirt shape onto the fabric from the template on page 136. Cut carefully around the outline.

3 Fold the card in half, and cut out the neckline.

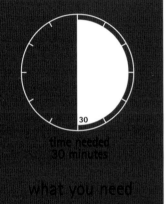

**time needed
30 minutes**

what you need

Thick white paper

Fabric scrap
(large enough for card)

Scissors

Glue

Pencil

10

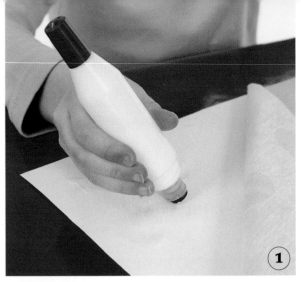
1

2

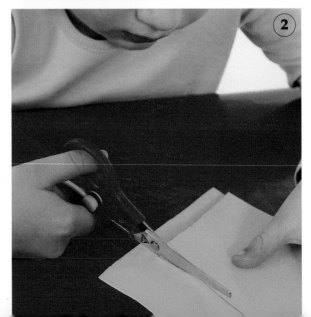
2

variations

• You can be really creative with these clothing cards. Either use the template provided, or make up your own shapes, such as a shoe with laces, or a baseball cap. Here are some ideas to try:

- Felt hat with sequins and feathers.
- Cotton apron with lace trims and pockets.
- Boxer shorts with buttons and ribbon.
- Bag with pompom and coloured pipe cleaners.

tips

★ Apply the glue to the paper rather than the fabric. Make sure you spread it evenly.

★ Don't be over-ambitious size-wise. It's easier to stick the fabric to a small area.

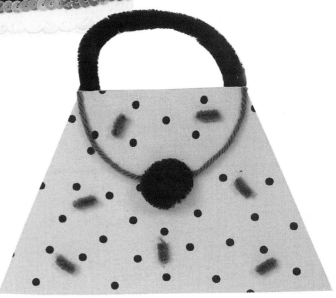

loved-up T-shirt

ages 5–6 years

Help your loved ones to wear their hearts on their chests by stencilling them a heart T-shirt. Any design looks stunning in silver textile paint, and you only have to iron it to fix the paint. The stencil can be used several times.

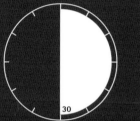

time needed
30 minutes

what you need

Paper
Pencil
Scissors
T-shirt
Iron
Sticky tape
Stencil paint
Brush

1 Make a stencil using the heart template on page 137 or by drawing half a heart shape on a folded piece of paper and cutting it out with scissors.

2 Iron the T-shirt flat. Place a piece of paper inside the T-shirt (to protect the back). Position the heart stencil on the front of the T-shirt and tape it down. Paint on the stencil paint gently with short dabs.

3 Remove the stencil when the paint is dry (if it dries flat you can use the stencil again). Iron to fix the paint, following the manufacturer's instructions.

1

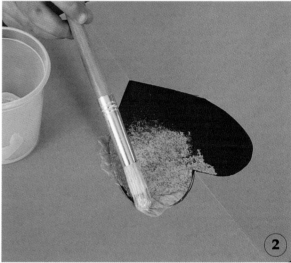

2

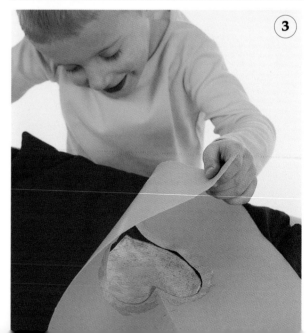

3

variations

love-lights

Add a touch of sparkle to your stencilled heart by using glitter fabric glue and heart *diamantés*.

sweetheart bag

Stencil a silver heart onto a piece of felt. Glue around the edges onto another piece of felt the same size and add glitter, sequins and a ribbon handle.

star socks

Make a pretty pair of socks look extra special by adding a tiny stencilled star motif embellished with glitter glue.

tip
★ Always test the stencil out first on a spare piece of fabric.

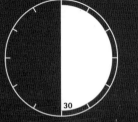

time needed
30 minutes

what you need

Purple corrugated card
Pencil
Scissors
Craft knife
Pink wool
Coloured beads
Blue corrugated card
Glue

sweetheart photo frame

ages 5–6 years

Simple shapes cut out of card with added decoration of wool and beads make unusual photo frames. If you place a special photograph inside the frame this makes a very special personal gift for Father's or Mother's Day.

1 Draw a heart on the purple card using the template on page 137. Cut it out using the scissors. Draw a smaller heart in the centre on the back of the card. Cut it out using the craft knife.

2 Cut a piece of pink wool and glue it to the front of the card around the cut edge of the smaller heart. Stick beads randomly onto the front of the heart.

3 Cut a square piece of blue card large enough to cover the smaller heart shape. You may need to trim the bottom corners to follow the shape of the heart. Apply glue to the sides and bottom of the blue piece and stick it down onto the back of the purple heart. The top edge should be left open to slot in the photograph.

4 To make the stand, cut out a rectangular piece of blue card and align one narrow edge with the centre of the top of the blue square. Glue it to the back of the frame so it can stand up.

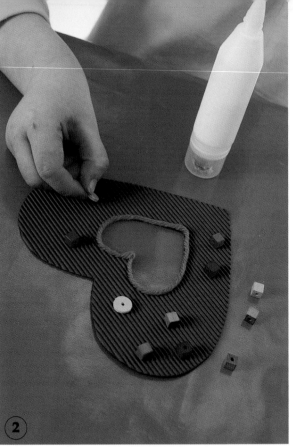

variations

square frame

This square frame is made more unusual by adding bands of contrasting strands of wool, tied and secured with a bead.

flower power

Make a flower-shaped frame in the same way and decorate with beads around the circular opening, threaded with wool knotted at the ends.

round frame

Wind wool in five different colours snugly around the frame, then decorate with wool ties and beads.

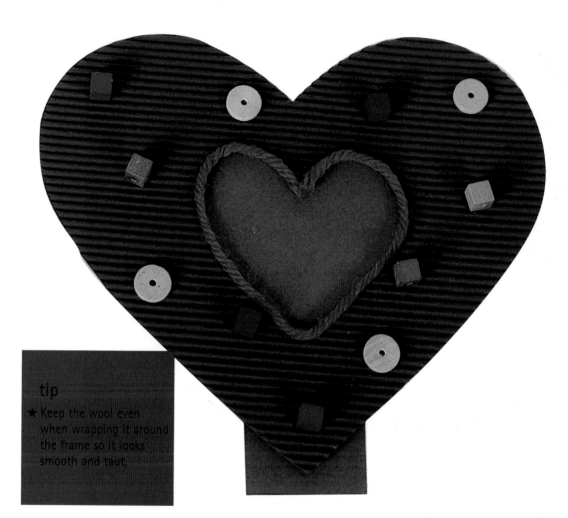

tip
★ Keep the wool even when wrapping it around the frame so it looks smooth and taut.

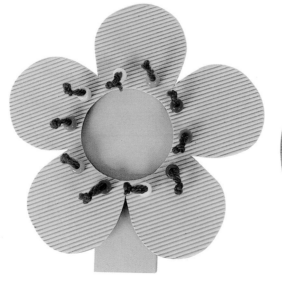

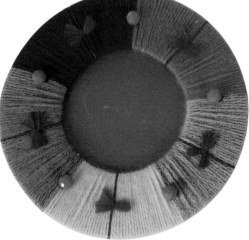

time needed
15–30 minutes

what you need

Scissors

Red paper

Pink heart-shaped
self-stick notes
(or pink paper)

Sequins and *diamantés*

Glue

valentine
cards

ages 2–6 years

Everyone loves to receive a special handmade card especially on Valentine's Day. There is something here for all the family to make. Furry pipe cleaners with folded arms and hands are great for the younger members, while the older children tackle the more sophisticated glitter hearts and lips. All the cards take only a few minutes to make.

1 Cut a red heart out of paper using the larger template on page 137.

2 Place a pink self-stick note in the centre of the card. If you cannot find these, draw and cut out a smaller heart from pink paper using the smaller template on page 137.

3 Fold the card in half so that it sits up on a flat surface.

4 Decorate with *diamantés* and sequins using dabs of glue.

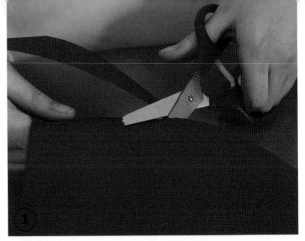

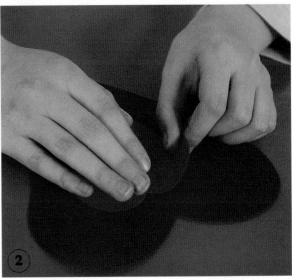

variations

hugs and kisses

Younger children will love making coloured hearts from pipe cleaners, with folded arms and hands glued on.

happy heart

Decorate a card heart with a face. Stick it onto a contrasting card at a jaunty angle. Add long folded legs with feet, for that special person in your life.

zigzag card

Stick decorated hearts to the top of twisted pipe cleaners and add them to the folds of a zigzag silver card for a multi-dimensional treat.

colourful flowers

ages 4–6 years

This cheerful selection of flower ideas for Mother's Day and Father's Day will keep children of all ages happy. Paper flowers are quick and simple to make. They can be glued onto a straw with a paper leaf and given with a gift, or made into a colourful bunch and arranged in a pot to be the gift itself.

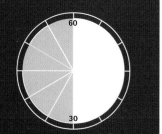

**time needed
30–60 minutes**

what you need

Green and yellow paper

Pencil

Scissors

Hole punch

Straw

Stick glue

Purple tissue paper

Ribbon

(1) Draw a leaf-shape on some green paper (fold the paper over several times to make several leaves at a time). Cut out the leaf. Punch a hole through the centre of the leaf and thread onto a straw. Stick the leaf to the straw with a dab of glue.

(2) Cut three layers of purple tissue paper into a flower shape and punch a hole through the centre. Cut a small rectangle of yellow paper for the flower centre.

(3) Thread the flower shapes onto the end of the straw. Dab some glue onto the yellow centre and stick it to the top of the straw.

4 Tie a ribbon around the straw and use on its own or pop it into a pot with a selection of other paper flowers.

variations

floral cards

Paper flowers glued to a card or placed in the fold look very effective, yet are simple to make.

flower pots

Flower pots can be made from recycled yoghurt or plastic cups. Simply paint them or cover them with paper and fill with a gift or a bunch of flowers.

tips

★ Cut several layers of tissue or paper circles at a time and make a decorative edge.

★ You may need to use a dab of glue when threading flowers and leaves onto the straws. Remember that PVA-glue will dissolve the tissue paper.

vanilla fudge

ages 4–6 years

These no-cook fudge goodies gift-wrapped in a pretty, shaped box make a quick stylish present – just don't eat too many or you won't have enough to give away.

**time needed
30 minutes**
(plus overnight to harden)

what you need

175 g (6 oz) butter, softened

Mixing bowl

1 small can sweetened condensed milk – approximately 175 g (6 oz)

800 g (1¾ lb) icing sugar, sieved

Pastry board

Rolling pin

Wire rack

Tea towel

Chocolate buttons

Sweet cases

Star box or tissue paper nest

1 Put the softened butter into a bowl and stir in the condensed milk. Gradually add the sieved icing sugar.

2 When it is mixed together, turn the fudge onto a pastry board and knead until it is smooth and easy to handle.

3 Roll out the fudge with a rolling pin to a thickness of 1 cm (½ in) and cut it into strips and then into neat squares.

4 Put a chocolate drop onto some of the squares if you wish. Leave overnight on a wire rack covered with a tea towel to harden.

5 Place the squares in sweet cases and pop in a box or make a nest of tissue paper.

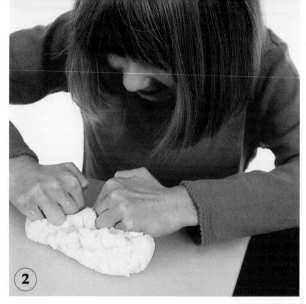

variations

other flavours

Experiment with different flavours by adding a few drops of vanilla or peppermint essence to the fudge mixture. Or sieve 75 g (3 oz) of cocoa with the icing sugar to make chocolate fudge.

chocolate hearts

Use a small heart cutter and make lots of fudge hearts or make a giant one that can be wrapped individually in cellophane.

tips

★ If the mixture is too thin, add more sieved icing sugar.

★ Roll the fudge out smoothly otherwise the surface will look cracked.

★ Use a dab of icing to stick the chocolate buttons (or other cake decorations) to the fudge squares.

ladybird gift tag

ages 2–6 years

Handmade paper tags will make any gift extra special and they can be made by children of all ages. Recycled food cans filled with bright spring flowers or bulbs make wonderful Mother's Day gifts; you can tie the gift tag onto a leaf or flowerhead.

1 Fold a piece of red paper in half. Draw half a ladybird shape onto the paper – a plump semicircle with a slightly pointed end. Cut it out.

2 Use the black felt-tipped pen to draw a line down the middle for wings and colour in the head.

3 Roll about eight small balls of black tissue or crêpe paper and glue them onto the ladybird.

4 Punch a hole through the head of the ladybird and thread a ribbon through it for the tag.

time needed
30 minutes

what you need

Red paper

Pencil

Scissors

Black felt-tipped pen

Black tissue or crêpe paper

Stick glue

Hole Punch

Red ribbon

1

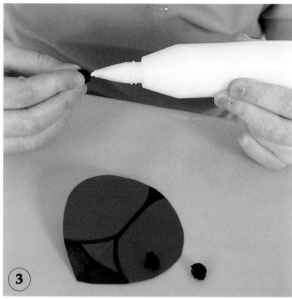

3

4

variations

• You can make tags in a variety of shapes and sizes: butterflies, bees, fish and flowers, for example. Use contrasting torn paper and tissue paper for decoration.

tips

★ Simple distinctive shapes work best and give quick results, especially satisfying for younger children.

★ Always fold card or paper in half then cut out shapes to ensure a symmetrical outline.

★ Paper is very strong. Try rolling it to make different shapes to glue onto your tag.

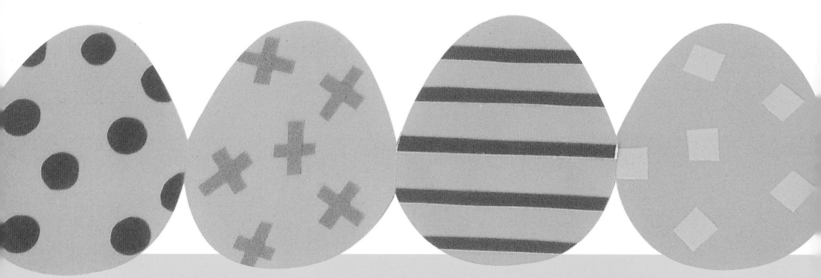

easter

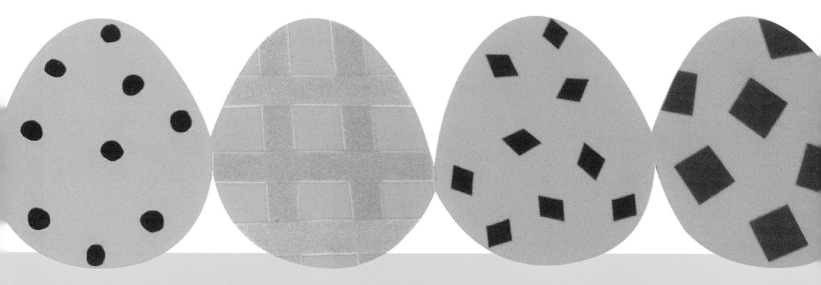

easter egg bunny

ages 2–6 years

These decorated eggs make an ideal gift for children to give to brothers and sisters, parents or grandparents on Easter Sunday.

1 To blow your own eggs, take a pin and pierce either end of the egg (this is a delicate operation and should be performed by an adult or with adult supervision). Blow through the top hole with a straw until the contents have run out, then rinse thoroughly with cold water and leave to dry.

2 Paint the eggs and leave to dry. You may need a couple of coats to cover completely.

3 While the paint is drying, cut out felt shapes for the ears, whiskers, nose, eyes and mouth.

4 When the paint is dry, glue the ears into position, folding back the lower end so that they rest on top of the egg. Glue on whiskers, eyes, a nose and mouth. Leave to dry.

5 Dab a little glue on the end of the plastic straw and insert the tip through the bottom of the egg and leave to dry.

6 As a finishing touch, tie a ribbon around the top of the straw and add a felt flower between the ears or at the front of the neck.

30

time needed
30 minutes

what you need

12 large eggs, if using real ones (to allow for breakages) or 6 plastic or polystyrene eggs

Large pin

Paints and paint brushes

Scissors

Felt

PVA glue

Glass beads or buttons

Plastic drinking straw

Narrow ribbon

(4)

(4)

(6)

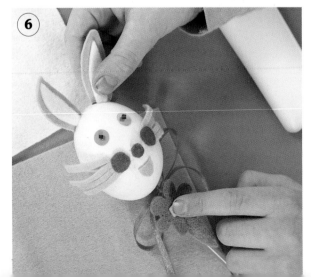

variations

jewelled eggs

These are simple but effective – choose sequins, glass beads or whatever takes your fancy and simply stick them onto the painted eggs. Thread a piece of ribbon through the holes and tie a knot at the bottom so that you can hang up the eggs.

jelly eggs

If you wish, you can fill the blown eggs with liquid jelly, then leave them in the refrigerator overnight to set.

tips
★ You can buy egg-blowing kits from craft catalogues or buy ready-blown eggs from garden centres.
★ To make paint stick to the eggshells, mix it with a little washing-up liquid.

funny faces

Instead of painting the eggs, leave the shells plain to mimic skin tone. Use wool or straw for the hair and stick on buttons, felt or pipe cleaners for the features.

candy bags

ages 4–6 years

These decorative baskets can be filled with any sort of candy or a small gift and wrapped or tied in a little piece of coloured net.

1 Take a square of yellow paper and cut along one edge with zigzag scissors. Form the basket shape by wrapping the zigzag edge of the paper around the bottom half of a beaker placed upside-down on the table. Tape the seam together and fold the free section of the paper over the bottom of the beaker to make the base of the basket. Secure with tape.

2 Cut a small strip of paper to be used for the handle using zigzag scissors and staple into position on each side of the basket.

3 Using ordinary scissors, cut a small fan-shaped piece of paper for a tail (don't forget to cut in the feathers) and two small wings. Glue the tail to the back of the basket, and the wings to either side, just beneath the handle.

4 Make eyes, a beak and a tuft of head feathers out of felt or paper and glue them onto the pompom head. When they are dry, glue the head onto the front of the basket.

5 Buy chocolate-covered eggs or other small gifts. Wrap them in a small piece of net, tie with a bow and place inside your bobtail basket.

**time needed
30 minutes**

what you need

Yellow paper

Scissors: zigzag and ordinary

Beaker

Sticky tape

Stapler

Glue

Yellow pompom for head

Felt or paper for eyes and beak

Chocolate eggs or small gift

Net

Ribbon

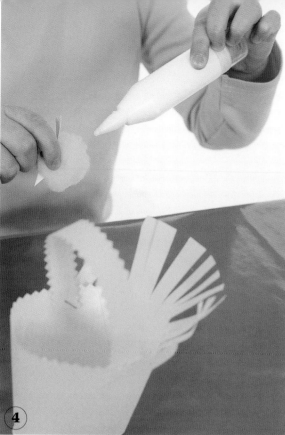

(4)

(5)

variations

• Making different shapes and animals makes this project fun for all the family. The baskets can be any shape or size but try and stick to an Easter theme, keeping the colours soft and pretty.

• Look out for boxes, bowls and anything that will make an interesting shape to use as a mould for your baskets.

tip

★ Make sure the paper is secured properly at the base of the basket and that the handles are secure.

flowery bonnet

ages 2–6 years

A decorative hat is a must for all Easter celebrations. Conjure up something bright and cheerful by using scraps of paper, zigzag scissors, feathers, beads and ribbons. It was once customary to wear something new on Easter Sunday, so why not make a hat for each member of the family?

1 Draw a circle on yellow paper, using a large plate to draw around. Cut out the circle and then cut a line into the centre of the circle. Fold the paper round to make a conical hat. Check it on the child (or adult) for head size, then staple the sides together.

2 Make six to eight large pink paper flowers and the same number out of purple paper. Use flower-shaped self-stick notes, if you can find them.

3 Glue a pink flower on top of a purple one, making sure their petals don't overlap completely. Punch a hole through the centre of each flower. Attach pairs of flower around the brim of the hat.

4 Thread a ribbon through a flower on each side of the hat, to go under the chin, and secure with a knot.

30

time needed
30 minutes

what you need

Pencil

Yellow paper

Large plate

Scissors

Pink and purple paper
(or flower-shaped
self-stick notes)

Hole punch

Stapler

Ribbon

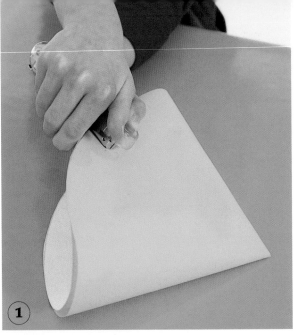
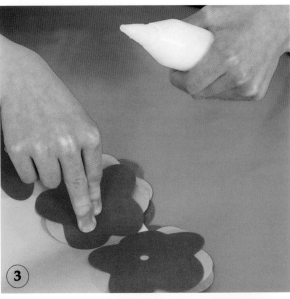

variations

folded bonnet

The folded bonnet has a cut decorative edge top and bottom with cut circles threaded with ribbon and knotted on each side. Decorate with pre-cut flower shapes or cut your own – the bonnet can be tied around the head or secured with hair grips.

hat bands

A broad strip of coloured paper decorated with flowers and feathers makes a quick stylish hat. Either staple the band together neatly overlapping or cross over at the front. Cut a circle into a spiral and stick only one end onto the band so the other hangs away from the hat.

tip

★ Use a small plate as a template for a small hat or a larger plate for a larger bonnet.

polka dot rabbit card

ages 2–6 years

Make a simple, brightly decorated, stamped card to give to friends and family at Eastertime. You can make stamps by cutting up vegetables such as potatoes and carrots or cutting a shape out of a sponge, or simply buying ready-made stamps from an art shop. This is fun and easy to do, as long as you don't mind the mess!

**time needed
30 minutes**

what you need

Orange card

Scissors

2 small potatoes

Knife or apple corer

Poster paint (four
     different colours)

Brush

Black felt-tipped pen

1   Using the template on page 138, cut a rabbit out of orange card.

2   Cut the potatoes in half and on each half score a small circle with a knife (or an apple corer) and cut away around it to leave a raised circle.

3   Use four contrasting colours of poster paint, one for each potato circle. Dab paint onto the potato circles with a brush and stamp over the orange card.

4   When the paint is dry, fold the card in half, then fold each edge back towards the middle fold so the card can stand up. Draw on a face with a black felt-tipped pen.

3

3

4

variations

coloured cards and tags

Stick a contrasting strip of paper onto a folded card. Cut out your stamped image and glue it into the centre of the card. Decorate with beads and sequins. Make a tag by threading a ribbon through a punched hole.

tips

★ Make a circle stamp by cutting a carrot in half and using the cut end.

★ Keep different coloured paints in separate containers and use a separate brush for each one so the colours stay bright and clean.

★ When stamping onto dark backgrounds, mix white paint into coloured paints.

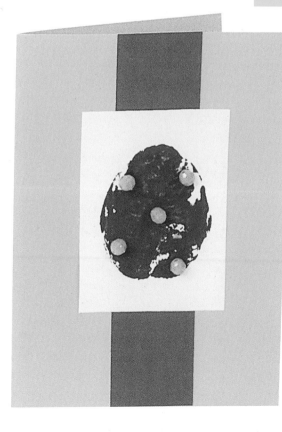

paper chick frieze

ages 4–6 years

Seasonal paper cut-outs make an ideal table or window decoration. They can be as simple or as complicated as you like: decorate just with felt-tipped pens, or more elaborately with cut paper, self-adhesive shapes, wool and ribbon. Wrap a frieze around a box and secure with sticky tape to decorate a gift, or cut off one of the shapes and glue it onto a folded card.

1 Take a long strip of yellow paper, about 70 cm x 10 cm (28 in x 4 in), and fold it evenly concertina style. You need six folds to give seven chicks, seven folds to give eight chicks, and so on. Make sure the folds align exactly.

2 Draw around the template on page 139, positioning the point of the beak against one fold and the base of the tail against the other. Cut out the chick, taking care not to cut through the folds at the beak tip and on the tail.

3 Unfold the frieze. Draw an eye and a wing on each chick with black felt-tipped pen and glue a feather on each tail.

30

**time needed
30 minutes**

what you need

Yellow paper

Scissors

Glue

Feathers

Black felt-tipped pen

Pencil

variations

egg extravaganza

Jazz up a simple egg frieze by decorating it
with coloured dots, beads, sequins and cut-out
squares and other shapes.

holding hands

This shape (see the template on page 138)
is a little more difficult to cut out.
Younger children can help to
decorate it by gluing on yellow
hair, making aprons from
net or a doily and
gluing on a waistband
and shoes.

tips

★ Use medium-weight paper or card
because lightweight paper tends to
curl when opened out.

★ Always make sure you don't cut the
folded edges.

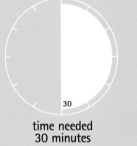

what you need

Polystyrene egg

Wooden skewer

Paint

Brush

Scissors

Coloured pipe cleaners

Glue

Elastic

Bead

hanging chickens

ages 2–6 years

These Easter chicks look very sweet hanging at a window or from a twig or plant. Make them in different sizes either by cutting them out of paper or using polystyrene eggs. Polystyrene eggs are great for younger children to paint and pipe cleaners can be pushed into them easily to make features, legs and tails. Beads, sequins and coloured feathers are ideal for further decorations.

1 Push a wooden skewer into the base of the egg, then paint the egg bright yellow, holding onto the skewer. Anchor the skewer until the paint has dried.

2 When dry, cut up coloured pipe cleaners: two blue bits for the eyes, orange for the beak and comb, brown and black stripes for the legs and tail. Push the eyes, beak and comb into position.

3 Thread a bead onto a length of elastic or string, securing it with a knot. Make a hole in the top centre of the egg with a skewer and glue the bead into it.

4 Push in pipe cleaners for the legs and tail.

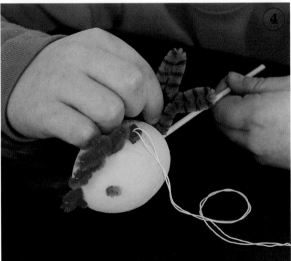

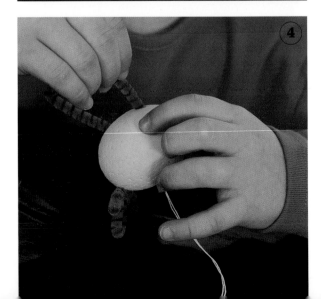

variations

changing chicks

To change the look, paint polystyrene eggs in different colours and decorate with feathers and beads. Hang on Easter twigs.

paper chicks

Make paper chicks by drawing your own template. Decorate them with feathers, use threaded beads for the legs or simply colour them with crayons.

chocolate cornflake crunchies

ages 4–6 years

time needed
15 minutes

what you need

100 g (4 oz) margarine

100 g (4 oz)
  marshmallows

100 g (4 oz) caramels
  (toffee-like sweets)

1 tablespoon drinking
  chocolate

Saucepan

Mixing bowl

200 g (7 oz) cornflakes

Wooden spoon

Coloured paper cake
  cases

Candy-coated chocolate
  beans to decorate
  (or other sweets)

Easter is a time for chocolate treats. These delicious easy-to-make cakes can be used for parties, teatime, or any special Easter event. Decorated with iced flowers, candies, eggs or chicks, they look good enough to give as a gift or to make for all the family during the Easter holidays. The biggest problem is to making sure they don't get eaten as soon as they are made!

1 Heat the margarine, marshmallows, caramels and drinking chocolate in a pan until melted and smooth. Add more drinking chocolate to taste if you wish. Pour onto the cornflakes and mix carefully with a spoon.

2 Spoon the mixture into paper cases making sure not to put too much into each case.

3 Sprinkle with candy-coated chocolate buttons or other sweets while still warm.

variations

rice pops with egg and flowers

Make the mixture as before, but leave out the drinking chocolate and add rice pops instead of cornflakes. Decorate each cake with a chocolate egg and shop-bought iced flowers.

tips

★ Always put decorations such as candy-coated chocolate buttons and chocolate eggs on the cakes when the mixture is still warm to ensure they stick.

★ If you can't find coloured cake cases, colour your own with felt-tipped pens.

crispy chick cakes

Shape the mixture into a small peak in the paper cases and pop a chick or egg, or any other decoration you fancy, on the top.

halloween

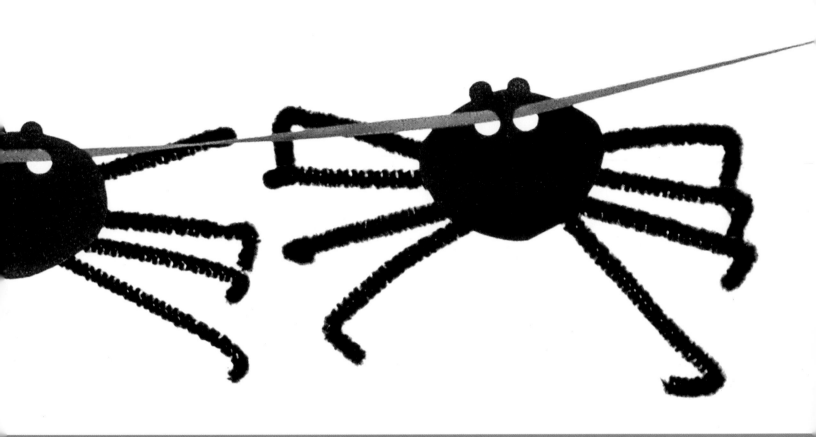

finger puppets

ages 4–6 years

These delightful finger puppets are easy to make as there is no sewing involved and they work well on little fingers for a party, or trick or treating. There are endless Halloween characters and animals to choose from and everyone from the youngest in the family to grandparents can join in the fun of creating a spooky character.

1 Cut out two rectangular pieces of black felt large enough to fit your finger, with a glued seam on either side. Glue three sides together, leaving the bottom open for your finger.

2 Cut a face out of the green felt and glue it on. Cut out a black hat.

3 Cut out black eyes, a nose and a mouth and glue them onto the face. Cut some strands of grey wool for hair and glue them into position.

4 Finally, glue the hat onto the head and decorate the face and hat with glitter glue.

time needed
30 minutes

what you need

Scissors

Black and green felt

Glue

Grey wool

Glitter glue

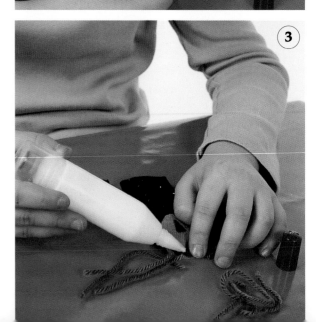

variations

monsters

Zigzag scissors make good decorative edges for a pumpkin or skeleton. Simply make the basic finger shape and add heads, arms and legs with puff paint or felt-tipped pens.

mouse

This cute mouse is made from a wedge of felt glued to form a cone. Decorate with eyes, wool whiskers and pink felt ears and nose.

dracula

Use red glitter felt for the body and glue on a black cloak. Make a green felt face and decorate with hair, eyes, eyebrows and fangs.

tip
★ Glitter felts are particularly effective at Halloween.

scary
skeleton

ages 5–6

Glow-in-the-dark paint and glitter work brilliantly for a trick or treat party, or whenever the lights are turned out. The paint and sparkle goes a long way so, it's ideal for several friends to have a go at creating decorations or their own scary skeleton T-shirt.

1 Draw bone shapes on white paper: ten sausages for ribs, seven rough circles for back vertebrae and elbows, and four traditional cylinders with a bulb at each end for the arms. Cut them out and position them on the front of the T-shirt. Tape them down so they don't move. Draw around the shapes with a white pencil.

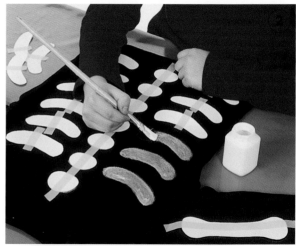

2 Remove the sticky tape and paper bones and place a piece of paper inside the T-shirt to make sure the paint doesn't go through to the back of the fabric. Paint the shapes with white fabric paint.

3 When the paint is completely dry (leave it overnight to be sure), lightly paint over the bones with glow-in-the-dark paint. Add a second coat of paint for an even better effect if you wish.

**time needed
1–2 hours**
(plus overnight to dry)

what you need

White paper

Pencils (ordinary and white)

Scissors

Black T-shirt (preferably long-sleeved)

Sticky tape

White fabric paint

Paint brush

Glow-in-the-dark paint

44

variations

night sky

Glittery glow-in-the-dark stars, moons and planets (use the templates on pages 134 and 140), are very effective party decorations. Simply fasten them on a wall or window with sticky tape or hang them from a piece of cord.

party invitations

Make a party invitation by sticking your motif to a card and complete it with glow-in-the-dark writing. Give clear instructions on the envelope that it must be opened in the dark.

tip
★ Use low-adhesive tape for sticking decorations to walls so that no damage occurs.

skull mask

ages 4–6 years

Paper plates are an ideal surface for children to decorate and they make excellent masks. Let your imagination run wild and create a unique Halloween mask for your fancy dress costume: perhaps a scary monster, witch's cat or a pumpkin face.

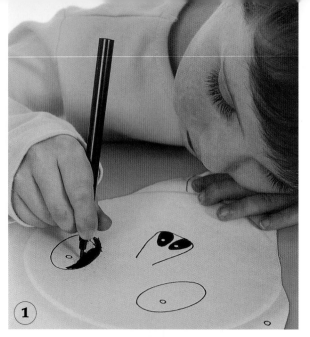

1 Draw a skull with hollow cheeks on a paper plate. Hold the face up to your own and get someone to mark where the holes for the eyes and nose should be. Also mark small holes on either side for the elastic cord. Using a black felt-tipped pen, shade in the eyes, nose and mouth.

2 Cut around the nose and pierce the eyes (if scissors are too big, ask an adult to help you do this with a knife). Use a hole punch to open the holes at the side of the mask for elastic to go through.

3 Make the top part of the jaw from a piece of the embossed edge of the paper plate that you have cut away. Glue it in place above the mouth. Knot one end of the elastic cord and thread it through a hole, check it for size and knot the other end through the second hole.

**time needed
10–30 minutes**

what you need

White paper plate

Pencil

Scissors

Knife

Black felt-tipped pen

Elastic cord

variations

witch's cat

For a black cat, make a half mask, paint it black and add a pink paper nose and long whiskers.

scary monsters

Make pumpkin and monster masks by gluing crêpe paper over a plate and sticking on scrunched up bits for warts. Decorate the masks in any sludgy colour you like with felt-tipped pens and glitter glue. (Remember to use stick glue for crêpe paper.)

tip
★ Choose lightweight paper plates as they are easier to handle and wear.

wizard's hat

ages 4–6 years

A ghoulish costume is essential for Halloween. If you haven't much time, a glittering wizard's hat and a simple black cloak should do the trick.

1 Mark the centre of the black paper with a pencil. Tie the string to the pencil and pin the other end of the string to the centre of the paper with a drawing pin. Hold the pin in place with your thumb and, keeping the string taut, draw a half circle. Cut out the shape.

2 Make a cone with the paper and try it on your child's head for size. Staple the sides together.

3 Draw different sized stars onto black paper with a white pencil using the templates on page 134. Cut out the star shapes, spread them with glue and sprinkle with plenty of glitter.

4 Glue your glitter star shapes evenly all over the wizard's hat.

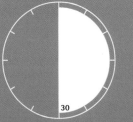

**time needed
30 minutes**

what you need

Black paper

Pencil

42 cm (17 in) string

Drawing pin

Scissors

Glitter

Glue

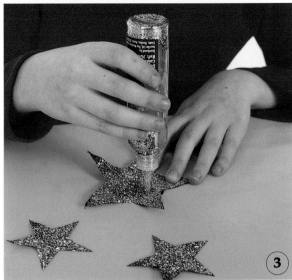

variations

bug bangles

Plastic creepy-crawly insects are perfect to make bangles and necklaces with. Just twist them on to sparkly pipe cleaners. They only take seconds to make and will be greatly admired on the night.

tip

★ Buy a big bag of plastic bugs: friends and family will love making things with them!

little devil

Furry devil head bands are just the thing for younger children.

carved pumpkins

age 5–6 years

Halloween wouldn't be complete without a carved pumpkin face to put on your doorstep with a lighted candle inside. Look out for the smaller varieties of squashes and gourds as well: these take very little time to cut out and make pretty lanterns on Halloween night or for a party.

**time needed
15–20 minutes**
(depending on pumpkin size)

what you need

Pumpkin

Knife (or craft knife)

Spoon

Black felt-tipped pen

Twigs

1 Cut the top off the pumpkin and scoop out the flesh with a spoon. Scrape out as much flesh from the sides of the pumpkin as you can, as the thinner it is, the easier it is to carve.

2 Draw a scary face on the pumpkin with a black felt-tipped pen. Cut out the features with a knife (or craft knife).

3 Make small holes in the top of the pumpkin and stick twigs in them to make hair.

variations

different colours

Squashes and gourds of varying sizes and colours can be decorated with simple holes made with an apple corer or a skewer.

different shapes

Draw star and flower shapes on a pumpkin with a black felt-tipped pen and cut them out with a craft knife.

IMPORTANT! Be very careful with lighted candles. Do not leave them burning unattended and remember not to put the pumpkin top on when a candle is lit otherwise it will start cooking and burn.

**time needed
30 minutes**

what you need

Black paper

White pencil

Scissors

Silver and black pipe
    cleaners

Sticky tape

Black cotton

Orange wool or beads
    for eyes

giant insect

ages 2–6 years

Hanging spiders and insects, ghosts, eyeballs and all the horrible things you can think of will all add to a Halloween party atmosphere. Simple cut-outs of giant creepy-crawlies and paper ghosts require little skill to make. The eyeballs may take a little longer, but whatever you choose to make, all ages will have plenty of fun.

1 Fold a piece of black paper in half. Using the template on page 139, draw half a beetle shape onto the paper with a white pencil and cut out the shape with scissors.

2 Place four silver pipe cleaners into position on the underside of the back for the legs and a black one for the feelers. Stick them down with tape. Make a small hole in the centre of the back and thread through a length of black cotton. Tie it in a knot to secure.

3 Make a small hole at the tail end of the beetle and thread through a piece of black pipe cleaner. Bend the legs to make the beetle stand up. Stick on orange wool or beads for the eyes and the ends of the feelers.

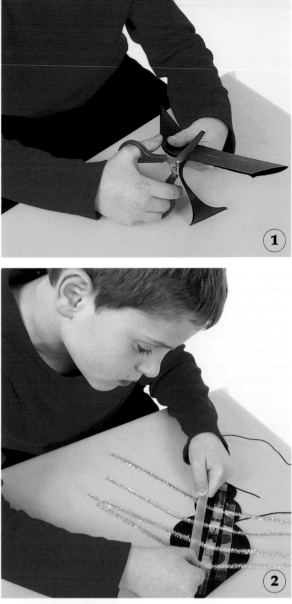

variations

dangling eyeballs

Make a ghoulish hanging with polystyrene balls decorated as eyeballs. Pierce a hole in the polystyrene ball, apply some glue to the hole and thread in a piece of cord. Leave to dry before using.

incey-wincey spiders

Black cut-out spiders threaded onto ribbon will look especially creepy at a window.

tip
★ Pipe cleaners come in various colours and sizes and are great for making creepy crawlies.

halloween invitations

ages 4–6 years

Halloween parties are always exciting, especially as there are so many spooky delights to make for them. Stick to a colour scheme of black and orange and keep all the family busy and amused preparing party bags, cards and invitations for the special day.

**time needed
15 minutes**

what you need

Black paper
White pencil
Scissors
Silver glitter glue
Orange corrugated card
Glue

1 Fold a piece of black paper in half. Using the template on page 141, draw half a bat shape on the folded paper with a white pencil. Cut it out.

2 Make the eyes with silver glitter glue. Fold each wing back towards the centre fold.

3 Unfold the bat and glue the tip of each wing to each side of a folded orange piece of corrugated card. Make sure the centre fold of the bat is on the centre fold of the card.

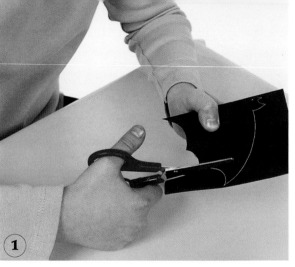
1

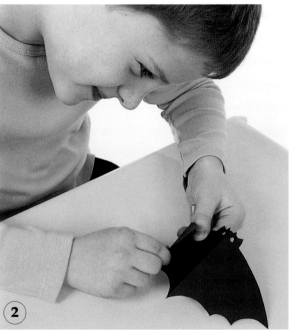
2

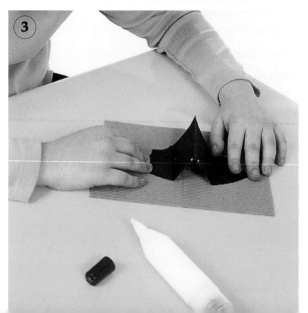
3

variations

party bags

Decorate small cones with black cut-outs of a cat's head (using the template on page 141). Make a sack from a length of crêpe paper folded and glued (using stick glue) along three sides; decorate it and fasten with wool, adding a slimy clip-on frog.

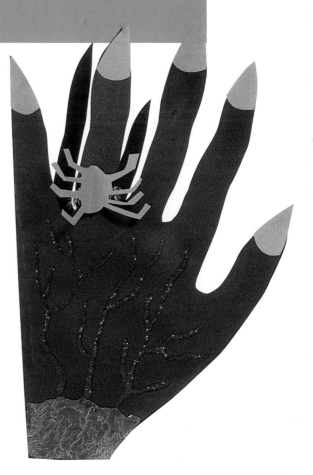

tip
★ Use a glue stick on crêpe paper – water-based glues dissolve and discolour the paper.

more scary cards

A simple black pumpkin (using the template on page 141) face will look stunning glued onto an orange card. Cut out a gruesome hand and give it glitter veins and spider ring (using the templates on pages 140 and 141).

bat biscuits

age 4–6 years

Biscuits are always popular and these bat-shaped ones are no exception. They are great for a party and make wonderfully appropriate trick or treats. Get everyone to have a go at creating a template of some creepy creature or shape.

1 Melt the butter, syrup and sugar in a saucepan, stirring until smooth. Mix the flour, bicarbonate of soda and spices in a mixing bowl, then stir them into the pan, adding the beaten egg and enough milk to make a smooth dough.

2 Preheat the oven to 180°C/350°F/Gas Mark 4. When the dough is cool enough to handle, knead and roll it out on a lightly floured surface to a thickness of 5 mm (¼ in). Cut out as many biscuits as you can with a bat-shaped cutter (or cut around your own card template with a small knife). Transfer to a greased baking sheet.

3 Make holes in the top of each biscuit with a skewer. Bake for 8–10 minutes in the preheated oven until the dough begins to darken. Remake the holes in the biscuits while they are still soft and leave to cool.

4 Meanwhile make the icing. Mix the icing sugar with a little black food colouring then gradually add warm water. Once the biscuits are cool, use a knife to cover each biscuit with icing. Before the icing dries, sprinkle each bat with edible bronze glitter.

time needed
45 minutes
(plus cooking time)

what you need

For the biscuits:

75 g (3 oz) butter

3 tablespoons golden syrup

150 g (5 oz) light muscovado sugar

Saucepan

375 g (12 oz) plain flour, sieved

2 teaspoons bicarbonate of soda

1 teaspoon ground ginger

1 teaspoon ground cinnamon

Mixing bowl

1 egg, beaten

1–3 tablespoons milk

Pastry board

Rolling pin

Bat-shaped biscuit cutter (or card template and knife)

Baking sheet

To decorate:

275 g (9 oz) icing sugar, sieved

4 tablespoons warm water

Black food colouring

Edible bronze glitter

④

variations

• Make a selection of different shaped biscuits and decorate them with orange, black and white icing, glitter shapes and liquorice strips. Make your own creepy templates to use instead of biscuit cutters.

④

tip

★ Edible glitter colours come in small pots, but a little goes a long way. A small pinch is sufficient to cover an iced biscuit.

thanksgiving
& harvest
festival

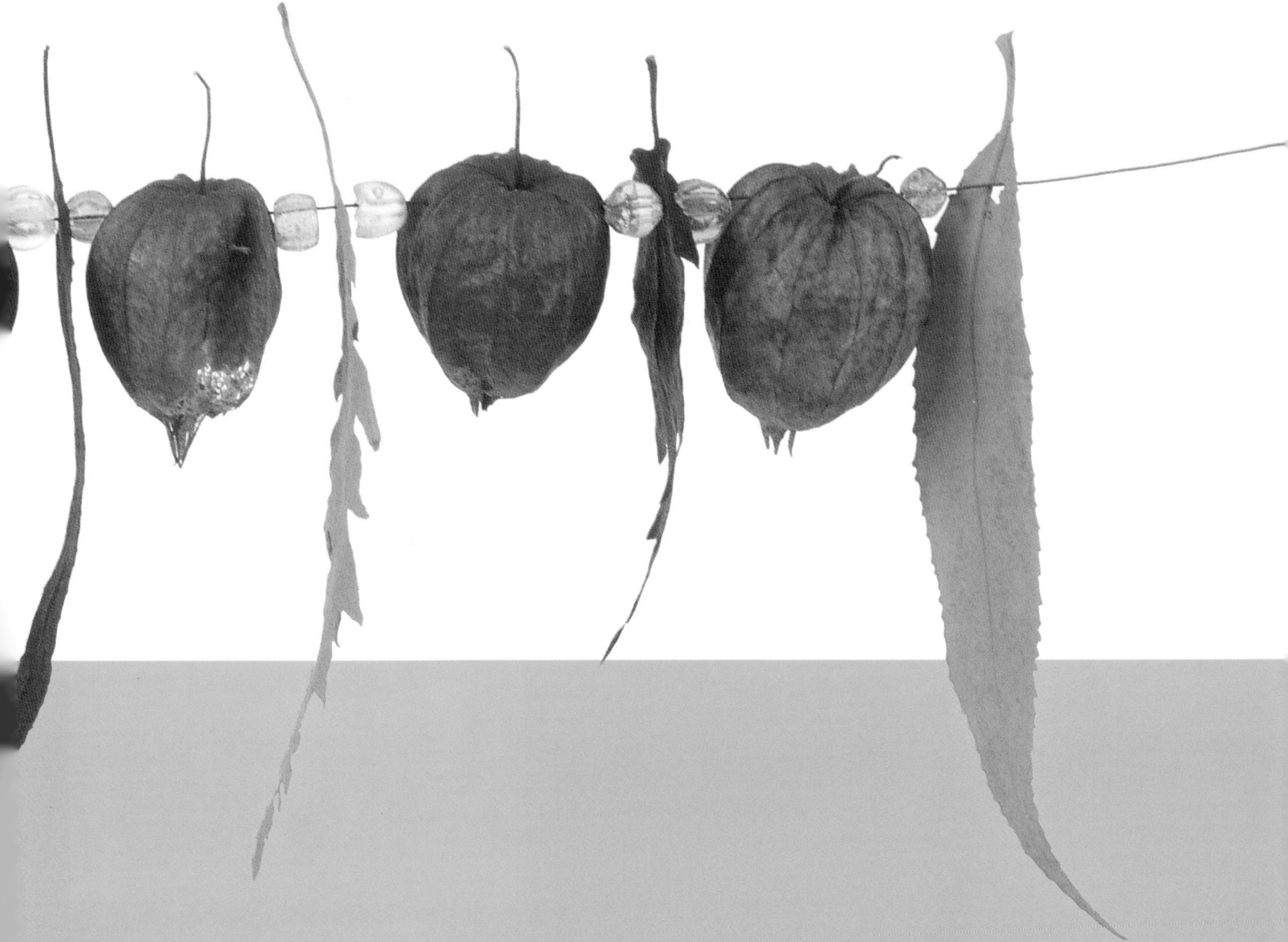

festive trees

ages 2–6 years

These bright colourful tree gifts are ideal for a party, Harvest Festival celebration or Thanksgiving dinner. The simple cones can be decorated according to your chosen theme and the bases filled with sweets or a small treat.

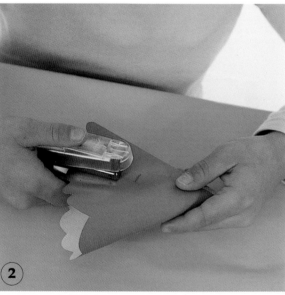

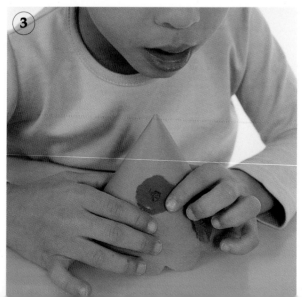

(1) Paint the cardboard roll green, then when it is dry paint on brown stripes. While the paint is drying, make a semicircle on the green paper by drawing around the edge of a plate. Cut a decorative border around the edge of the circle.

(2) Fold the semicircle into a cone shape, ensuring the top is pointed. Staple or tape edges together to make the tree canopy.

(3) Cut several layers of tissue paper into small circles. Scrunch up contrasting coloured tissue into small balls and glue to the circle centres to make flowers. Stick the flowers on to the cone.

4 Fill the base with sweets or a small treat, seal with tissue paper, then place the cone on top.

time needed
1 hour

what you need

Cardboard roll, about 10 cm (4 in) long

Poster paints and brush

Green paper

Pencil

Plate

Scissors

Stapler (or sticky tape)

Coloured tissue paper

Stick glue

Sweets (or small treat)

variations

snowflake and glitter tree

Make Christmassy-looking tree gifts using a tall cone from silver paper decorated with white sequins and glitter glue, or cover a red tree cone with white origami snowflakes.

tips

★ Cones can be given all sorts of different looks: play around with folding the paper till you get the shape you want.

★ Glue the cone tops to the roll to make them more secure.

★ Fill the base with sweets, then 'seal' with a ball of tissue paper.

fantasy tree

Create a fun tree with a zigzag edge by adding sequins, torn paper, net, or anything else you fancy!

autumn leaf tree

Cut out leaves in autumn colours and stick them onto a brown cone for a traditional Harvest Festival look.

feathered headband

ages 4–6 years

Why not make a headband for every member of the family to wear for a themed Thanksgiving dinner? They will look especially good when matched with the colourful table decorations given in the variations. Feathers can be bought or made from paper, and more details added in the form of scraps of paper, ribbon and beads.

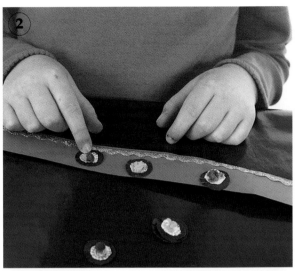

1 Mark out a strip 3 cm x 60 cm (1½ in x 24 in) on a piece of orange paper and cut it out. Stick gold rickrack braid along one long edge.

2 Make decorations from contrasting coloured circles of paper and silver paper with scrunched up tissue glued to the centre. Stick them at intervals along the band.

3 If you have some real feathers, use them. If not, you can make some out of coloured paper. Draw a long pointed oval with a stalk at one end. Cut it out, then make lots of small cuts all the way around the edge. Tape them sticking up at even intervals along the inside of the band.

4 Measure the band around the child's head, trim it to size if necessary and staple together to form the headband.

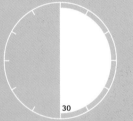

**time needed
30 minutes**

what you need

Pencil

Ruler

Coloured paper (orange and other colours)

Scissors

Rickrack braid

Silver paper

Tissue paper

Stick glue

Feathers (optional)

Sticky tape

Stapler

variations

placemats and napkin holders

Make placemats by simply cutting a piece of corrugated card to size, and gluing on a feather motif. For the napkin holders, cut a cardboard tube and cover with coloured paper. Add beads and feathers to decorate.

tip

★ Make different versions of the headband with tissue, ribbons and sequins. Any colourful scraps will look attractive, so feel free to experiment.

turkey place card

The turkey features strongly at Thanksgiving, so it makes a good motif for place cards. Draw a turkey, cut it out and colour it in. Stick onto a piece of folded card.

63

leaves and lanterns

ages 2–6 years

Celebrate the changing of the seasons by making decorations from dried leaves and flowers. Paint them and combine them with pretty glass and plastic beads and use them to decorate your house around harvest time.

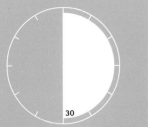

**time needed
30 minutes**
(plus 2 weeks to dry leaves
and lanterns first)

what you need

Leaves (or dried leaves)

Newspaper

Heavy books

Chinese lanterns
   (*Physalis*) (or dried
   Chinese lanterns)

Poster paint

Beads

Garden wire

(1) Collect attractive autumn leaves. Place them flat between eight sheets of paper (newspaper is fine) and press down with books. Leave in a warm dry place for two weeks. Allow sprigs of Chinese lanterns to dry naturally in a vase.

(2) Paint pressed leaves, choosing autumn colours. Pick off the Chinese lanterns carefully from the stems when they are dry.

(3) Thread leaves, beads and Chinese lanterns onto garden wire to make a hanging decoration.

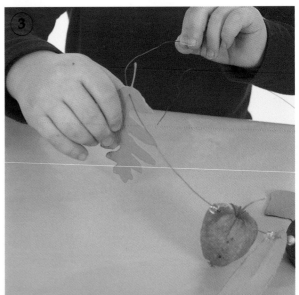

variations

hanging decorations

Thread a painted leaf and bead onto a short piece of wire and twist the wire to form a loop.

candleholder

Decorate a candleholder with painted leaves and a wire threaded with coloured beads.

tip

★ Choose brightly coloured leaves to press, so that you won't need to paint them.

time needed
30 minutes

what you need

Dried stalks of grass,
  corn or grain

Garden wire

Scissors

Red wool

Glue

Lace

Ribbon

Fabric

Beads

Heads of grain

corn dolly

ages 5–6 years

These corn dollies are made from stalks and ears of grain. They are very decorative for the home and can be made by adults and children alike. Small children can participate by tying a bundle together with a pretty ribbon as a gift for a teacher or friend.

1 Take a small bundle of stalks approximately 15 cm (6 in) in length. Starting a little below the top, twist two pieces of garden wire around the bundle to mark off the head.

2 Immediately below the bottom wire, separate a few strands on each side for arms. Trim these to an appropriate length, and secure each one with a little wire around the wrist area. Wrap some red wool around the wires and fasten it.

3 Make a dress by gluing lace and ribbon onto a small rectangle of fabric. Wrap it snugly around the doll and glue the seam down the back.

4 Glue on small dark beads for the eyes and tuck decorative heads of grain into the wool headband for additional decoration.

variations

boy dolly

Make a boy dolly in the same way, but separate the bundle at the bottom for legs. Make a masculine costume from scraps of fabric and ribbon.

bundle of corn

Simply tie a few stalks together, trim the ends and decorate with ribbon and fabric. This decoration can be hung or stood on a table.

tips

★ When buying bundles of grain make sure it is not too dried out as it breaks easily.

★ Even tiny scraps of fabric and ribbon can be used for decoration.

corn plait

Secure one end of a bundle to a table with tape. Plait it and twist into a shape, then tie with a ribbon and tuck in some decorate heads of grain: it's as simple as that.

heart of corn

Take two small bundles of equal length and plait them. Bend the pair into a heart shape and tie the two joins together with wire. Decorate with ribbons and a tiny bell.

potato heads

ages 3–6 years

This is a fun idea for a party or even to take as your gift for the Harvest Festival. Before raiding the refrigerator for fruit and vegetables make sure you ask first, then use whatever you can find – you will be amazed how many different faces you can make!

1 Push cocktail sticks into all the vegetables so you can stick them in the potato. Cut the cocktail sticks in half if they are too long. First press two kumquats into the potato to make feet.

2 Cut a piece of corn to use for a nose. Then stick two blueberries above the nose for eyes and cut a radish for the mouth.

3 Place a mangetout on each side of the potato for earrings.

4 Add a few leaves of sprouting broccoli or cabbage for the hair and top with a broccoli floret.

time needed
30 minutes

what you need

Cocktail sticks

Scissors

Knife

Large potato

2 Kumquats

Baby sweetcorn

2 Blueberries

Radish

2 Blueberries

2 Mangetout

Sprouting broccoli
    or cabbage

2 Mangetout

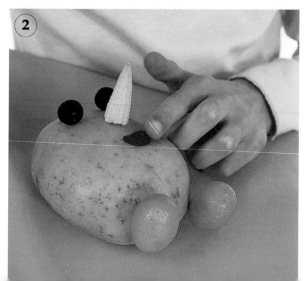

variations

- Give a sweet potato green feet made from spring onion stalks. Add radish eyes and a blueberry nose and top with kale hair and a kumquat and bean hat.

- Add rings of carrot for legs to a large baking potato. Cut out mangetout lips, radish eyes and an onion nose. Make a hat with mushroom and onion and secure it to kale hair.

- Create a colourful character out of a red potato with courgette feet, a carrot nose, corn eyes and blueberry ears. An onion-stalk hat can be decorated with aubergine.

tips

★ Only make these characters immediately before they are needed – keep them outside and spray with water to keep fresh.

★ Use a cut-down skewer at the back of the potato to help it stand up.

salt-dough butterfly

ages 4–6 years

Salt dough is easy to make and exciting for kids to model with. Create bright and colourful decorations for the table or give them away as gifts.

**time needed
1–2 hours**
(plus 6 hours cooking)

what you need

Mixing bowl

Spoon

2 cups plain flour

1 cup salt

1 cup tepid water

Rolling pin

Pastry board

Butterfly cutter (or cardboard template)

Cocktail stick

Baking sheet

Greaseproof paper

Glue

Poster paint (yellow and other colours)

Paint brush

1   In a mixing bowl, mix the flour and salt, then add the water gradually until the dough is firm. Knead the dough for about 10 minutes, then leave it to rest for 40 minutes at room temperature.

2   Roll out the dough to 5 mm (¼ in) thick on a pastryboard. Add a little extra flour if the dough or the rolling pin becomes too sticky.

3   Cut a butterfly shape with a cutter (or cut around a cardboard template). Use a cocktail stick to decorate with small holes. Make a hole at the base for the stick once the butterfly is cooked.

4   Place the butterfly on greaseproof paper on a baking sheet. Heat the oven to 120°C/250°F/Gas Mark ½ and bake for about six hours, until it is hard and looks completely dried out.

5   Allow the butterfly to cool – it should be rock hard – then insert a cocktail stick into the hole with a dab of glue. Paint the butterfly with yellow poster paint. and add more detail with paint in other colours.

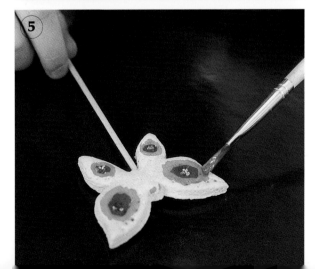

variations

animals and flowers

You can make all sorts of shapes using biscuit cutters, or design your own, such as the leaf here, and make cardboard templates to cut around. Decorate them using different coloured paints.

christmas

tree treats

ages 2–6 years

These special parcels make attractive Christmas tree decorations and are great mini-gifts for adults and children alike. Wrap a small present in tissue paper and place it inside the tree bag or pop in some colourful sweets or chocolates.

1 Cut two identical Christmas tree shapes out of green felt.

2 Place one piece of felt on top of the other and glue an orange pipe cleaner at the top of the tree between the two layers of fabric. Continue to glue around the edges then press the pieces together. Leave to dry.

3 Glue sequins, beads and fun shapes onto the front of the tree. Place a pompom or star at the top. Leave the glue to dry.

4 Thread a small section of pipe cleaner or wool through the holes in the beads. Dab with glue to secure.

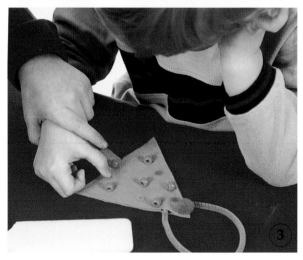

5 Cut a slit in the back of the tree so that the gift can be popped inside.

**time needed
20 minutes**

what you need

Scissors or pinking shears

Green felt

Assorted pipe cleaners

Sequins

Beads

PVA glue

Pompom

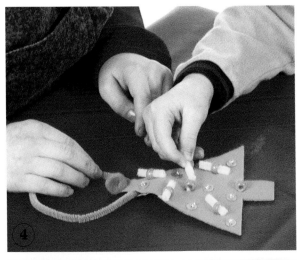

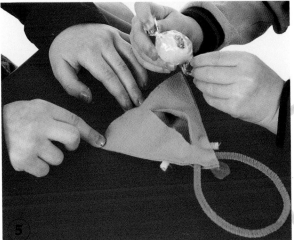

variations

all that glitters

If you want a sparkly tree bag, use tinsel and glitter and design a reindeer using the template on page 134.

hearts and stars

You can cut a variety of shapes in different colours, depending on the occasion, using the templates on pages 134–135.

tip

★ Do not use too much glue or it will ooze out and spoil the felt.

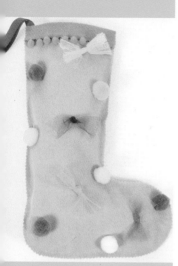

christmas stocking

ages 5–6 years

Christmas for children isn't complete without a stocking. These unusual decorated examples can be made with adult help, but all embellishments should be left for children to do. Materials such as felt and net ensure the stockings are quite strong and should last for several Christmases to come.

1 Draw the stocking template on page 135 onto a double thickness of felt. Cut out two stocking shapes with zigzag scissors.

2 Apply glue along the edges of both stockings (except the tops). Carefully press together. While the glue is drying, make several net bows in different colours by tying a knot in a small piece of net.

3 Glue the bows and pompoms evenly all over the stocking. Cut out and stick on a hanging loop and a felt band in a contrasting colour along the top edge. Add a pompom trim below the band.

30

**time needed
30 minutes**

what you need

Turquoise and pink felt

Pencil

Zigzag scissors

Glue

Coloured net

Coloured pompoms

Cord or ribbon
(for hanging loop)

Pompom trim

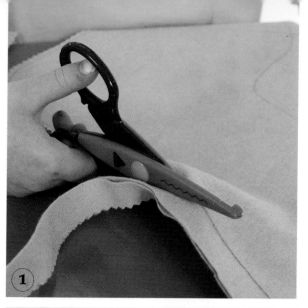

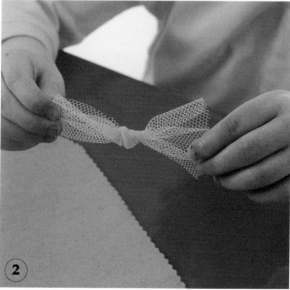

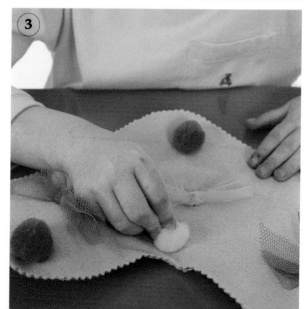

variations

cut-out shapes

For a more sophisticated look, cut a star shape out of the felt and glue contrasting coloured net to the back. Stitch both stocking shapes together with a running stitch and trim with brightly coloured beads.

tip

★ Don't fill your stocking with heavy gifts.

see-through stocking

Stitch together stocking-shaped pieces of net with wool and trim with ribbon, plastic beads and wired-on felt. These stockings look especially effective with brightly coloured tissue-wrapped parcels inside.

advent calendar

ages 5–6 years

Why not make your own Advent calender and fill each felt pocket with a tiny trinket or sweet?

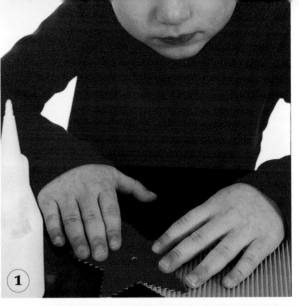

1 Cut a tree shape out of the green card. With zigzag scissors, cut out a pink felt star (see page 134 for template) and glue to the top of the tree. Punch a hole through the centre of the star.

2 Use the small tree, heart and star templates on pages 135–135 to cut out 24 shapes from different-coloured felts (with ordinary scissors).

3 Draw 24 oblong shapes – 2.5 cm x 7 cm (1 in x 3 in) – on different coloured felts. Cut them out with zigzag scissors. Apply glue to the long edges of the felt oblongs, fold over and press together to make a small felt bag.

4 With puff paint or a marker pen, write the numbers 1 to 24 on small foam shapes. Glue each one onto a felt shape and then glue the felt shapes onto the little bags.

5 Place the Velcro base dots onto the tree at even intervals. Place the other halves of the Velcro dots onto the underside of the 24 felt bags. Insert the trinkets or sweets into the felt bags and press into place on the calendar. Thread a cord through the hole at the top.

**time needed
2–3 hours**

what you need

Green corrugated card, 50 cm (20 in) square

Pencil

Scissors (ordinary and zigzag)

Coloured felts

Hole punch

Glue

Three-dimensional puff paint, available from art shops (or marker pen)

Foam shapes

Velcro dots

24 trinkets or sweets

Cord

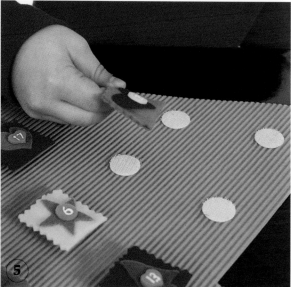

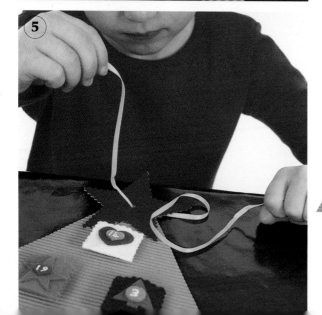

tips

★ Use ready-printed numbers for speed.

★ Substitute chocolates for the felt pockets on the tree, if you are short of time.

variation

chocolate calendar

Tape ribbon loops to the back of 24 Christmassy chocolate shapes. Write the numbers 1 to 24 on small adhesive dots and stick one onto each chocolate. Peg the chocolates up in order on a length of decorative ribbon.

3-D paper decorations

ages 2–6 years

Paper decorations look so attractive hanging at the window or on a tree. Three-dimensional ones are particularly effective hanging where they will be seen from all sides. An alternative to these three-dimensional stars is snowflakes made out of origami paper. It's always fun to unfold a snowflake and such a surprise to see how it looks!

1 Fold a sheet of coloured card in half. Draw a star on it using the template on page 134. Cut around it to get two stars. Decorate both stars with glitter glue.

2 Cut one star from a point to its centre. Make a cut in the other star from between two points to its centre. Align the cuts and slide the stars together to make a three-dimensional shape. Pierce a small hole through the point where the two stars meet and thread the cord through to make a hanging loop.

**time needed
30 minutes**

what you need

Coloured card
  (or thick paper)

Pencil

Scissors

Glitter glue

Pin

Cord

variations

different shapes

You can make angels, Christmas trees or baubles. Decorate them with stars and glitter or use two different coloured papers.

origami snowflakes

Fold a square piece of paper in half, then quarters and then into a triangle. Draw a pattern along both folded edges and then carefully cut out the snowflake shape. Unfold, flatten out and peg onto a cord.

tip

★ Three-dimensional decorations need heavy paper or thin card, or they will curl up. Snowflakes need thin paper such as origami or tissue paper, or they are too difficult to cut out.

rocking cards

ages 2–6 years

Handmade cards and gift tags are inexpensive to make and a must at Christmas. Younger children will love these rocking Christmas cards, while coloured bands to wrap around boxes, and tags attached to brightly coloured ribbons will make any gift look special. Decorative punches with many designs can be bought from art shops and give hours of pleasure as they are so easy to use.

**time needed
30 minutes**

what you need

Scissors

Coloured paper

Star punch

Silver star

(**1**) Cut a circle out of coloured paper (draw around a small plate to make a template) and fold it in half. Punch stars around the edge of the semicircle.

(**2**) Cut out a star (see page 134 for template) in another colour. Stick it to the middle of the folded edge with glue.

(**3**) Add a silver star to the centre of the star.

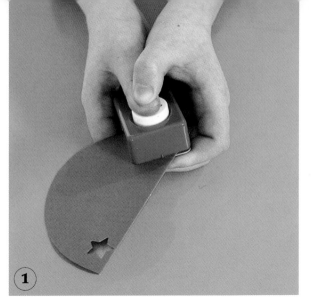

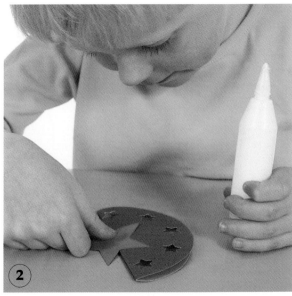

variations

design your own card

Customize rocking cards for any occasion by sticking different shapes on to the fold. You can use the templates on pages 134–135 for Christmas shapes.

wrap it up

Make inexpensive gift wrap by covering a box in coloured paper and adding a contrasting band with glued on trees or other decorations.

gift tags

Tags are so quick to make if you use lots of different shapes and coloured papers. Simply punch and stick for an amazing variety.

tips

★ Pre-cut shapes such as self-stick notes make cards and tags even quicker to assemble.

★ Use bright, contrasting coloured papers for the best effect.

festive snowman

ages 4–6 years

Made out of air-drying clay, these sparkly snowmen make excellent gifts and are good enough to keep from year to year, either as tree decorations or for a Christmas table (attach them to napkins with ribbon). Once you've made and dried the shapes, encourage everyone to get together to decorate them.

1 Place the clay on a pastry board and roll it out to a thickness of 3 mm (⅛ in). Smooth lightly with water to keep the clay flat. If you have a snowman cutter, use it to cut out the shape, or cut around your own cardboard template with a knife. Make a small hole in the hat to thread ribbon through.

2 Leave the snowman to dry overnight, turning to keep it flat.

3 If the clay is not white, paint it with white poster paint. Allow to dry, then put glue on the hat and sprinkle on the silver glitter. Carefully draw on a face and scarf.

4 Use the red glitter for the scarf, and glue on a bead for the nose. Finally, thread a red ribbon through the hole in the hat and fasten it to make a hanging loop.

**time needed
30 minutes**
(plus overnight to dry)

what you need

Air-drying clay

Pastry board

Rolling pin

Snowman cutter (or cardboard template)

White poster paint

Silver and red glitter

Glue

Felt-tipped pens

Bead

Red ribbon

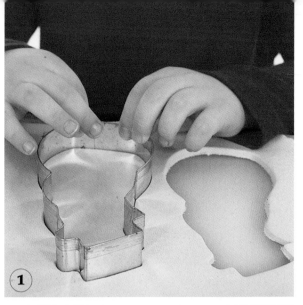

variations

glittering stars

Make star decorations in the same way as the snowman. You can use glitter glue instead of sprinkling glitter onto the glued surface.

beads and baubles

In fact, all sorts of painted decorations with beads and sequins glued on are quick to make. Don't forget to make holes through the clay before it dries with a pin for hanging loops, or to hang beads on the decorations.

tips

★ Try to buy white clay so that you don't have to paint it.

★ Keep clay airtight after use for future projects.

★ The painted decorations can be painted with watered-down PVA glue to give extra protection before decorating with sequins and beads.

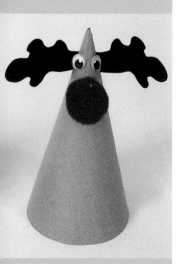

rudolph reindeer

ages 2–6 years

Cone decorations take minutes to construct and can be made into any character you like; they are great fun for all the family to make. Give them away as gifts, use them as table decorations or simply hang them on the Christmas tree. You can decorate them with pre-cut shapes, glitter, paper and feathers as well as fabric scraps.

**time needed
30 minutes**

what you need

Plate

Pencil

Card (or stiff paper)

Scissors

Stapler (or sticky tape)

Black paper (or paper and crayons)

Glue

Wobbly eyes

Red pompom

1 Draw half a circle on a piece of card or stiff paper using the template on page 134 or by tracing around a plate. Carefully cut it out.

2 Make a cone shape out of the semicircle, then staple or tape it together.

3 Cut antlers out of black paper (or you could colour your own). Glue them onto the back of the cone near the top.

4 Glue the eyes onto the front.

5 Glue on a red pompom for the nose. Leave to dry.

1

3

variations

father christmas

Use red and white paper or card to make
a traditional jolly Santa Claus.

(4)

(5)

penguin

Glue on pompom eyes, a beak and
foam feet. Make wings out of black
paper and add a ribbon loop at the
back so you can hang it up.

tinsel and sparkle

A home-made fairy or wise king
on top of the Christmas tree will
look much more special than a
bought one. Glue glitter net
around a cone and add either a
halo or a crown.

tip
★ If you use pre-cut, self-adhesive foam
  or paper shapes there is no need to
  use glue.

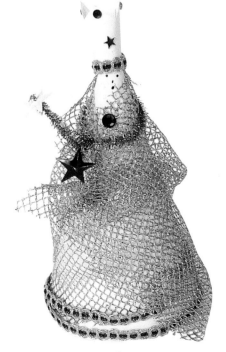

christingle candles

ages 3–6 years

Christingle oranges have a wonderfully spicy aroma. Cloves are relatively easy for little fingers to push into an orange, just make sure to protect the surfaces from the juice! It's easy to make lots of interesting patterns and the oranges look especially attractive with candles in them either for use at home or for the Christingle service at church.

1 Cut several cocktail sticks in half and push each one through a cranberry. Decorate your orange with a line of cranberries, pushing one in at a time.

2 Add two lines of cloves to the orange, above and below the cranberries.

3 Use an apple corer to scoop out the centre of the orange and place a candle in the hole (this is best done by an adult).

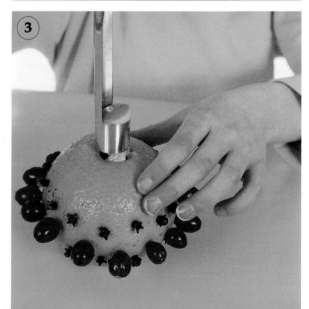

**time needed
30 minutes**

what you need

Cocktail sticks

Scissors

Cranberries

Orange

Cloves

Apple corer

Candle

variations

• Try making different patterns on your Christingle orange with circles or lines of cloves, or wrap a ribbon around it.

gingerbread decorations

ages 2–6 years

Gingerbread cookies are very festive for this time of the year. If you can possibly resist eating them, hang them on the Christmas tree or wrap them up to give as a gift.

1 Preheat the oven to 180°C/350°F/Gas Mark 4. Melt the butter, syrup and sugar in a saucepan, stirring until smooth. Mix together the flour, bicarbonate of soda and spices and stir into the pan, adding the beaten egg and enough milk to make a smooth dough.

2 When the dough is cool enough to handle, knead and roll it out on a lightly floured surface to a thickness of 5 mm (¼ in). Cut out as many biscuits as you can with the gingerbread cutter (or use a small knife to cut around a cardboard template). Transfer to a greased baking sheet.

3 Bake the gingerbread cookies for 8–10 minutes in the preheated oven until the dough begins to darken. Remove from the oven and leave to cool.

4 Mix the icing sugar with the warm water. Decorate the surface with white icing and silver balls then draw on the detail with red writing icing. Allow the icing to dry and tie a narrow ribbon around the neck.

30

**time needed
30 minutes**
(plus cooking time)

what you need

For the gingerbread:

75 g (3 oz) butter

3 tablespoons golden syrup

150 g (5 oz) light muscovado sugar

375 g (12 oz) plain flour

2 teaspoons bicarbonate of soda

1 teaspoon ground ginger

1 teaspoon ground cinnamon

1 egg, beaten

1–3 tablespoons milk

Rolling pin

Pastry board

Gingerbread cutter (or cardboard template)

To decorate:

275 g (9 oz) icing sugar, sieved

4 tablespoons warm water

Red writing icing

Silver balls

Thin red ribbon

(2)

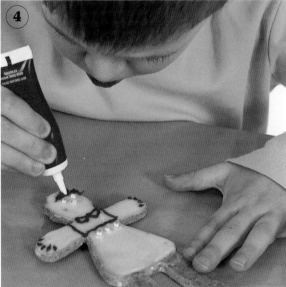

(4)

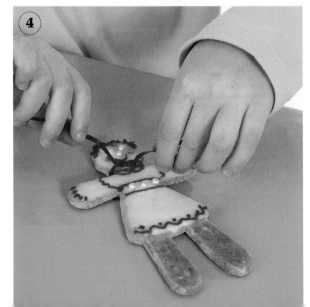

(4)

variations

all shapes and sizes

Using different shaped cutters will give great variety to your assortment of biscuits especially when they are decorated with coloured icing, iced stars and multi-coloured dots.

tip

★ Always pierce a hole in a biscuit before you bake it if you want to thread a ribbon through. Make it a good size as they can close up during cooking.

birthdays

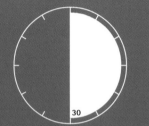

foam necklace

ages 5–6 years

Foam is safe and easy to use and gives hours of pleasure to all ages. It comes in sheets or pre-cut shapes in many colours. Badges, necklaces and bracelets make ideal gifts for sisters, friends and even brothers. Some pre-cut shapes have self-adhesive backing so there is very little mess and even younger children can have a go, too.

1 Draw four flowers and five leaf shapes onto foam using the templates on page 137. Also draw 12 small squares in several different colours.

2 Cut out all the shapes. Punch a hole through one end of the leaves. Punch a hole through the centres of the flowers and squares.

3 Thread the shapes onto a piece of chenille or ribbon, alternating the flowers and leaves with the small squares. Once all the shapes are threaded, tie the ends together to make the necklace the desired length. Trim the ends if necessary.

**time needed
30 minutes**

what you need

Pencil

Coloured foam

Scissors

Hole punch

Length of chenille or ribbon

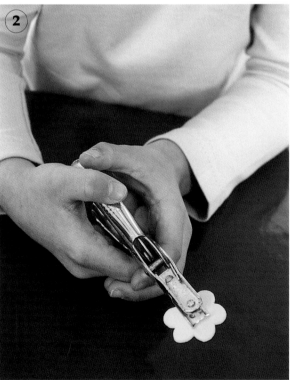

variations

easy necklace

Thread pre-cut shapes onto plastic cord, tying a knot in between each of the shapes.

bracelets

These take no time at all to make. Simply cut a foam strip (using zigzag scissors if you wish), decorate it by punching holes and tie together with strands of cut foam. You can also thread these strands through the holes.

badges

Use pre-cut shapes with plastic eyes to make a caterpillar, or be a bit more creative and cut a dog or cat shape to decorate as you please! Glue your badges to cardboard tags with a safety pins on the back, which can be bought from stationery stores.

paper crowns

ages 2–6 years

Hats made from plain or patterned tissue paper can be decorated with feathers, sequins, glitter glue and different types of paint. This easy project is fun for all ages and even very young children can share in the activity without too much mess. The great things about these hats is that you can cut out several at the same time. Have a 'party-hat party', where you let your friends decorate their own hat!

1 Cut a length of patterned tissue paper long enough to go around your head and fold it into quarters. Mark a zigzag along the top with a felt-tipped pen and cut it out.

2 Tape the sides of the hat together to fit your head.

3 Apply gold glitter glue randomly over the surface of the hat. Allow the glue to dry before you put the hat on.

time needed
5–10 minutes

what you need

Patterned tissue paper

Scissors

Felt-tipped pen

Sticky tape

Gold glitter glue

variations

• Look out for tissue paper in unusual colours or with unusual prints, or even reuse any that you are given.

• Cut out hats with different decorative edges. Coloured sticky tapes are a quick method of embellishing a hat.

• Glitter and sequins give a sparkle to plain tissue and feathers can be glued or stapled on. But only use lightweight sequins and feathers.

tip

★ Don't use water-based glues or paints as these dissolve tissue paper.

revolving letter card

ages 2–6 years

Personalize a birthday card or invitation by placing a number or letter on a contrasting background; attach it with a press stud or paper fastener through the centre so it revolves. Everyone loves to receive a handmade card, parents and grandparents alike. Keep colours clean and fresh and perhaps buy a bright coloured envelope to pop your card in.

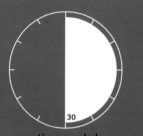

(1) Draw a large capital letter on a piece of purple paper and cut it out with scissors or a craft knife.

(2) Stick on pre-cut gummed shapes or flowers to decorate.

(3) Place the letter in the centre of a card in a contrasting colour, here green. Punch a hole through both the card and the letter and place the press stud into position.

**time needed
30 minutes**

what you need

Paper

Pencil

Craft knife or scissors

Pre-gummed shapes

Card

Hole punch

Stud or paper fastener

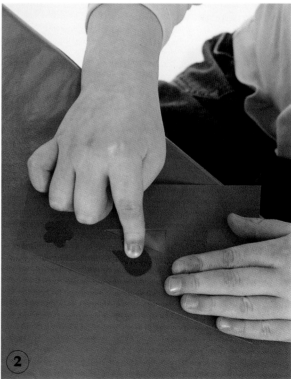

variations

- These cards can be made in all shapes and sizes. Make a round one and cut around the circle with zigzag scissors, or punch holes around the edge with a hole punch.

tip
★ Use pre-cut gummed shapes for quickness, but you can always design and stick on your own.

- Glue strips of patterned paper onto a plain card before adding your revolving shape.

- A teddy bear, robot, boat or any shape you fancy could be used instead of a letter or number.

gift wrap and tags

ages 2–6 years

Making colourful wrapping paper is a wonderful project for a fine summer's day. Lay your paper outside with pots of coloured paints and enjoy marking the paper with different brush strokes. You can also make tags out of the same decorated paper threaded with ribbon or chenille. If you do this projects indoors make sure you cover all nearby surfaces!

1 Dab paint circles onto plain coloured paper at even intervals. Leave to dry.

2 Make a gift tag by by cutting the painted paper to size. Glue the tag onto card if the paper is thin. Punch a hole for the tie to go through.

3 Make interesting ties from ribbon, chenille or pipe cleaners.

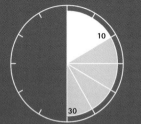

**time needed
10–30 minutes**

what you need

Poster paint

Rolls or sheets of coloured paper

Brushes

Scissors

Glue

Card

Ribbon, chenille or pipe cleaners

variations

- Contrasting colours work well for gift wrap. Try green and orange, bright blue or a paler blue background.

- Experiment with painting dots, squares, stripes and crosses.

- Make matching cards, paper, tags and envelopes using self-adhesive dots and stars.

tips

★ Decorate bought luggage labels for gift tags.

★ Always protect surfaces well when painting indoors.

★ Add a touch of white to some colours to give them more strength.

- Choose ribbons that make the colours look even brighter, such as day-glow green or pink.

clown cakes

ages 4–6 years

With all the excitement at a birthday party, a cake can often get overlooked. By making individual clown cakes, children can take them home without too much mess. Make them the day before the party so that the birthday boy or girl can direct and join in the all-important decorating.

1 Preheat the oven to 180°C/350°F/Gas Mark 4. Place all the cake ingredients in a mixing bowl and blend with a wooden spoon. You can process the mixture in an electric mixer if you prefer.

2 Spoon the mixture evenly into 12 gold cake cases. Bake the cakes in the preheated oven for 15–18 minutes. Remove and leave to cool on a wire rack.

3 Meanwhile, roll out the red icing. Use the biscuit cutter to cut circles of icing to fit the top of the cakes.

4 When the cakes are cool, spread the tops with apricot glaze and place the icing circles on top. Decorate with sweets and add a clown.

**time needed
30 minutes**
(plus cooking and cooling)

what you need

For the cake:

125 g (4 oz) soft margarine

125 g (4 oz) caster sugar

125 g (4 oz) self-raising flour, sifted

2 eggs

Mixing bowl (or electric mixer)

Wooden spoon

Gold cake cases

12-hole bun tin

Wire rack

To decorate:

Ready-made red icing (or icing sugar, water and red food colouring)

Round biscuit cutter (the same size as the top of the cake cases)

Rolling pin

Apricot glaze

Pastry brush

Sweets to decorate

Clown decorations on cocktail sticks

variations

• When making a batch of cakes for a party, use several different coloured icings and a mixture of small sweets and cake decorations.

• Instead of clowns, place a birthday candle or sparkler on the cake.

tip
★ If you are short of time, buy a cake mixture.

birthday bandannas

ages 5–6 years

These brightly patterned bandannas are a great idea for a children's birthday party. With special felt-tipped pens for use on fabric and stencils it doesn't take long to design a small piece of material. Younger children can participate by adding dots and lines, while you can write messages using the darker pens.

1 Iron the handkerchief into quarters, then open it out and use the creases to mark where to put the stencil. Draw around the stencil with a felt-tipped fabric pen.

2 Colour in the line drawing using the felt-tipped fabric pens.

3 Iron to fix the design, following the manufacturer's instructions.

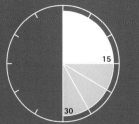

**time needed
15–30 minutes**

what you need

Cloth or handkerchief

Iron

Stencil

Coloured felt-tipped
fabric pens

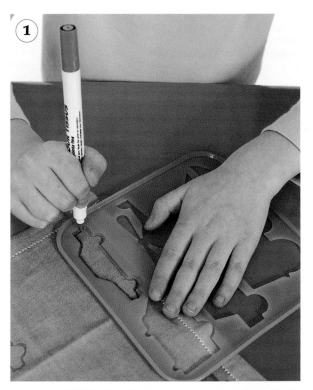

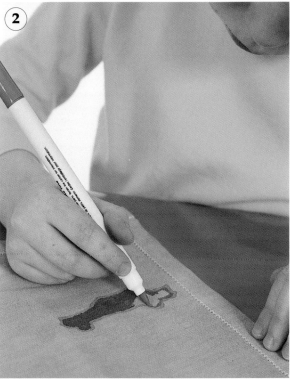

variations

fluorescent colour

Make an eye-catching border using a fish and star stencil and fluorescent felt-tipped pens. Go for a bright contrast such as simple dots of fluorescent pink on a dyed orange background.

teddy-bears' picnic

Have a bandanna party for all your teddy bears.

tips

★ Men's handkerchiefs make good-sized bandannas.

★ Try dying some white hankerchiefs for a colour background.

carnivals

hawaiian costume

ages 5–6 years

This costume conjures up the carnival atmosphere, especially if it's made in vibrant colours. You just need a sunny day to wear it! Crêpe paper is amazingly strong, so this no-sew outfit means that children can get help to make it.

1 Measure the child's waist and the length from waist to knee. Cut out a rectangle of these dimensions in each of the coloured crêpe papers.

2 Lay the papers flat one on top of another and clip them in place. Staple them along the top edge. Unroll a length of sticky tape, sticky-side up, on a table. Carefully place the stapled edge of the papers on half of the sticky tape, then fold over the other half, pressing it down firmly along the length.

3 Cut the skirt into strips of equal width, leaving a band of at least 2.5 cm (1 in) along the top uncut.

4 Punch a hole in each end of the sticky tape, and strengthen it with a hole reinforcement. Thread a ribbon through both holes to tie the skirt on.

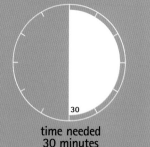

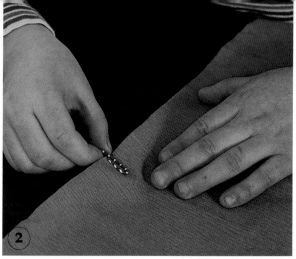

what you need

Tape measure

Crêpe paper in 4 colours (one must be yellow)

Scissors

Stapler

Wide, clear sticky tape

Hole punch

Ring reinforcements

Ribbon

variations

flowers in your hair
Make a paper flower to wear in the hair. Try one with a contrasting centre and a cut green leaf.

hair band
Glue different coloured flowers onto a hair band.

garland
Make flower garlands by threading cut-up coloured straws and circles of coloured paper or flower shapes alternately onto a ribbon.

glitter mask

ages 2–6 years

Masks act as a disguise, giving an air of mystery and excitement. These glittery masks can be as simple or as complicated as you wish. It's a good opportunity to use beautiful glitters, exotic feathers and an assortment of sequins and beads. Paper half-masks are especially good for young children to make and if time is short you can always decorate a bought one.

1 Fold the paper in half and draw half of your mask shape – the folded edge is the middle of your mask. Cut it out. Cut out the eyes and punch holes at the sides for the elastic cord, then reinforce them with a ring reinforcement or sticky tape.

2 Work on a surface that is easy to clean such as a plastic table cloth, or spread out newspaper for protection. Spread glue all over the mask. Sprinkle on different coloured glitters, covering the mask well. Allow to dry then shake off the excess.

3 Thread elastic through the holes at the sides of the mask. Knot securely after making sure it sits comfortably on the child's face.

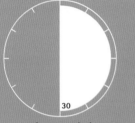

**time needed
30 minutes**

what you need

Strong paper or card

Pencil

Scissors

Hole punch

Ring reinforcements
 or sticky tape

Glue

Coloured glitters

Elastic cord

110

variations

choose a theme

Why not try an insect, harlequin or exotic eastern-looking mask. Decorate it using feathers, stick-on sequins, glitter paint and glitter glue.

ready-made masks

These make an instant disguise and can be decorated in numerous exciting ways. Try glitter stars, camouflage, zebra or leopard prints.

tips

★ Never use thin paper as it will tear.

★ Always strengthen the holes for elastic with ring reinforcements or sticky tape.

painted flags

ages 2–6 years

Handmade paper flags, chains and hanging decorations make a colourful display for any carnival. Once the paper has been decorated, it can be cut into all sorts of shapes and sizes and will look much more interesting than anything you can buy. This brilliant project is extremely messy, so it's best done outside in the garden on a fine day.

1 Lay sheets of paper on a protected surface (the lawn is perfect). Mix two or three colours of paint so it isn't too runny. Dip a brush into a paint and flick it across the paper. Clean the brush (or use another one) and do the same with the other colours, and on different coloured paper.

2 Make a template of a large triangle. Once the paint is dry, draw around the template onto the coloured paper and cut out flags.

3 Apply glue to the top edge of the flag, fold it over a length of string, and press with a finger and thumb to secure. Add the other flags to the string in the same way. Once the glue is dry, tie them up where the breeze will catch them.

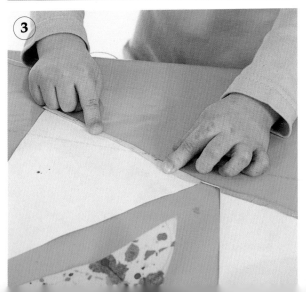

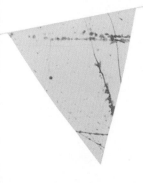

30

**time needed
30 minutes**

what you need

Coloured paper (several colours)

Paint (several colours)

Brush (or brushes)

Card for template

Pencil

Scissors

Glue

String

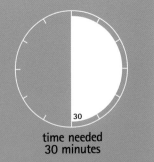

variations

paper chains

Paper chains are excellent for lots of children to make at the same time. Join them all up and see how long the chain is.

fringed flags

Cut the painted paper into small fringed rectangles as a good alternative to traditional bunting.

garden party

String up flowers with decorated centres and leaves.

tips

H Vary the thickness of the paint for a variety of effects.

H Always lay different coloured papers out at the same time and experiment with a selection of coloured paints.

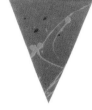

decorated candles

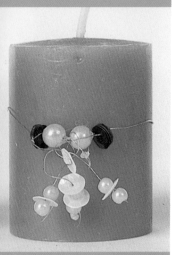

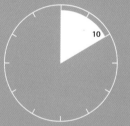

what you need
Candles
Garden wire
Scissors
Beads
Sequins

ages 3–6 years

Decorate these candles as a pretty gift or simply use them for a carnival celebration. Threading or gluing on beads is a very simple way of embellishing a candle. Even the youngest members of the family can contribute by helping to choose the beads and maybe by threading them. Look out for shaped sequins and unusual beads.

(1) Take a small piece of wire and thread with beads and sequins, placing a large bead in the centre.

(2) Thread some pearly beads onto a longer piece of wire. Pass the shorter wire through the pearls on the longer wire, leaving a small loop hanging down. Then add some red and pink sequins to the longer wire.

(3) Wrap the longer wire around the candle, twisting the ends to secure them.

(1)

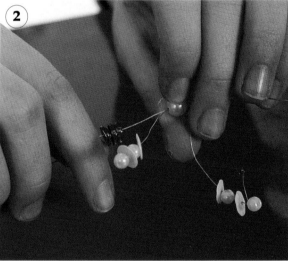

(2)

(3)

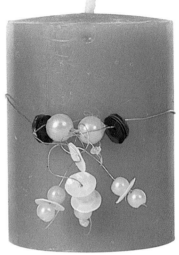

variations

sequin crazy

Hang pretty-shaped sequins from a wire or simply thread them on a wire and wrap it around the candle to give a stunning sparkly effect.

elegant candles

Make a gorgeous gift by gluing beads and glitter stars onto tall coloured candles and placing them in a box lined with tissue paper.

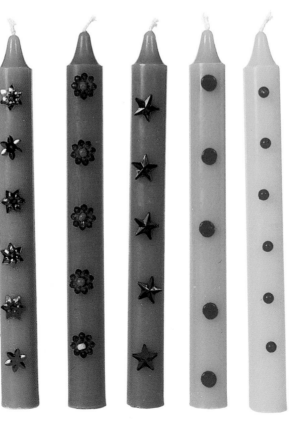

tip

★ When gluing on beads, keep the candle steady by placing tissue paper on each side. Leave to dry thoroughly or the beads fall off easily.

colourful bangles

ages 5–6 years

This fluorescent painted papier-mâché bangle will make a wonderful addition to any carnival costume. Although rather messy, this is an appealing project and the final results are well worth it.

1 Tear a newsaper into small pieces and place in a bowl. Mix three parts water to one part PVA glue to cover the torn newspaper. Leave overnight.

2 Squeeze the excess water out of the newspaper and add a little more PVA glue until you can begin to mould the papier-mâché.

3 Find a cardboard tube wide enough for a bangle. Cut it to the size you want with a craft knife. If you need to make it smaller, cut it and tape the edges together.

4 Begin placing papier-mâché pulp on the cardboard bangle. If it doesn't stick well, add more glue as you work around the bangle. Smooth the edges as you go around.

5 Leave the bangle overnight to dry. Paint with white poster paint as a base colour. When dry, you can mark the pattern with a pencil first if you wish. Paint on a blue zigzag pattern, add large pink dots and finish with yellow puff paint.

**time needed
45 minutes**
(plus 2 nights for drying)

what you need

Newspaper

Bowl

Water

PVA glue

To decorate:

Wide cardboard tube

Craft knife

Sticky tape

Pencil

Poster paints
   (white, blue and pink)

Brush

Three-dimensional puff
   paint

Ribbon

variations

papier-mâché beads

Make beads of all sizes out of papier-mâché and you can put together a host of different bracelets, necklaces and earrings. Remember to pierce a hole through the wet papier-mâché before it dries overnight. Paint these bracelets and necklaces in contrasting fluorescent colours.

4

5

5

earrings

Use the beads to make earrings by threading through elastic cord or fishing line.

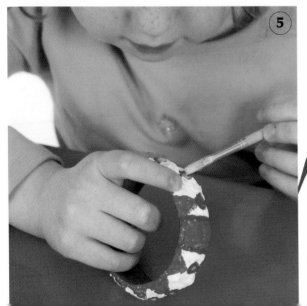

sparkling cakes

ages 4–6 years

A selection of decorated fairy cakes is always a treat for friends and family alike. Edible glitter looks wonderful and makes rather ordinary looking cakes and biscuits into something special and exciting. These cakes are perfect for a carnival party. Beware of the glitter: it goes everywhere and can stay on hands and face for hours!

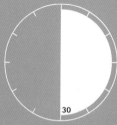

**time needed
30 minutes**
(plus cooking and cooling)

what you need

Cake mixture:

125 g (4 oz) soft margarine

125 g (4 oz) caster sugar

125 g (4 oz) self-raising flour, sifted

2 eggs

Mixing bowl (or electric mixer)

Wooden spoon

Plain paper cake cases

12-hole bun tin

Wire rack

To decorate:

Bowl

Spoon

225 g (8 oz) icing sugar, sieved

2–3 tablespoons water

Blue edible glitter

Foil parasol

Glitter glue, sequins for paper cases

Bowl and spoon

1 Preheat the oven to 180°C/350°F/Gas Mark 4. Place all the cake ingredients in a mixing bowl and blend with a wooden spoon. You can use an electic mixer if you prefer.

2 Spoon the mixture evenly into 12 paper cake cases. Bake in the preheated oven for 15–18 minutes. Remove and leave to cool on a wire rack.

3 Meanwhile, make the icing by mixing the icing sugar with the water. When the cakes are cool, spread the tops with icing.

4 Sprinkle each cake generously with edible blue glitter.

5 Decorate the paper cases with glitter glue and finish with a foil parasol.

1

3

tips

★ Sprinkle the edible glitter onto the icing before it has set.

★ Buy decorated cases if you don't want to make your own.

4

variations

glittering patterns

Sprinkle the glitter in lines, dots and criss-cross for different effects.

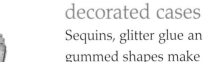

decorated cases

Sequins, glitter glue and pre-gummed shapes make a plain paper case look eye-catching – no one will be able to resist them.

festivals around the world

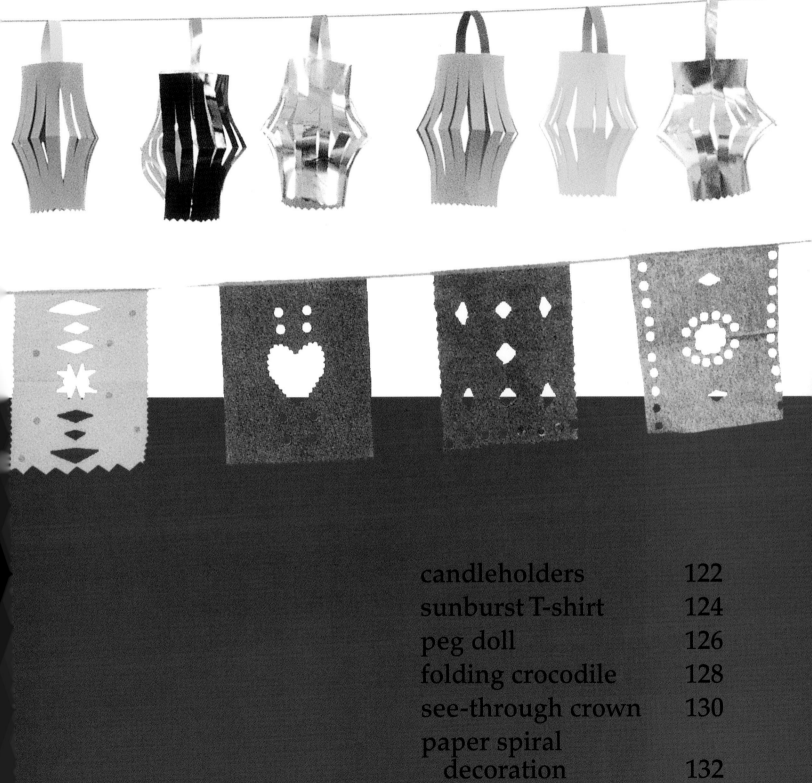

candle-holders

ages 4–6 years

Make these beautiful candleholders for family or friends for a special festival or enjoy them at home anytime. The coloured tissue paper gives a glowing vibrant colour, it's easy to apply and fun for children to decorate with sparkle, sequins and beads.

1 Choose the glass you are going to use and cut a piece of green tissue paper large enough to fit around it. Apply stick glue lightly to the paper and wrap it around glass. Press it against the surface so it sticks. Don't worry if the paper creases as this gives more interest when a candle is lit inside the glass. Trim any excess tissue paper from the top of the glass.

2 Cut small strips of turquoise tissue paper. Make the same number of cerise-coloured stars and dot them with glitter glue. Stick the stars to the tops of the turquoise strips.

3 Glue the non-star end of the turquoise strips along the inside rim of the glass then fold them over the edge so that the stars are hanging down. Put a candle in the glass.

**time needed
20 minutes**

what you need

Coloured tissue paper
Pencil
Scissors
Glitter glue
Glass
Stick glue
Candle

variations

• Try using tissue paper in clashing colours such as red and pink. Make decorative trims around the rim of the glass using sequins and torn paper. Decorate the sides of the glass as well.

• A blue tissue paper-covered glass embellished with silver sequin-braid and large flowers has extra sparkle.

IMPORTANT Be very careful with lighted candles. Always ask an adult to light the candles and never leave them unattended.

tips

★ Recycle glass jars and containers instead of buying glasses.

★ Night-lights are safer to use than ordinary household candles.

★ Remember that water-based glues will dissolve tissue paper.

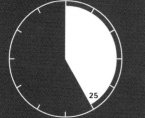

sunburst T-shirt

ages 5–6 years

Tie-dye on white fabric can produce brilliant colours and is an exciting way to brighten up old clothes or other pieces of fabric. Buy one of the tie-dye kits on the market, and all you have to do is follow the instructions.

**time needed
25 minutes**
(plus overnight to soak)

what you need

T-shirt (old or new)

Tie-dye kit (or cold water dyes, bottles, paint brush and fixative)

Rubber bands

Rubber gloves

Apron

Plastic bag

1 Wash the T-shirt and leave it damp. To achieve a sunburst effect, pinch up the centre of the fabric at the front and add rubber bands at intervals. Also pinch a small piece of material on each sleeve and secure them with more bands.

2 Wear rubber gloves and protect surfaces and your clothes. If using a kit, fill the bottles and paint sections according to the instructions given, either using the bottle or a dabbing on each section with a brush.

3 When you have applied the dye, place the T-shirt in a plastic bag, seal it and leave overnight for the dye to really soak in.

4 Wearing the rubber gloves and apron, take the T-shirt out of the bag and rinse it repeatedly in cold water until the water is clear. Wash it in hot water with soap, rinse and leave to dry naturally – away from any heat.

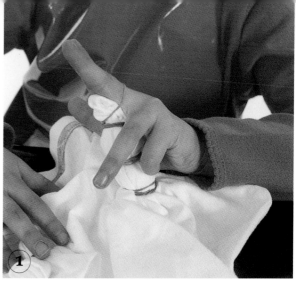

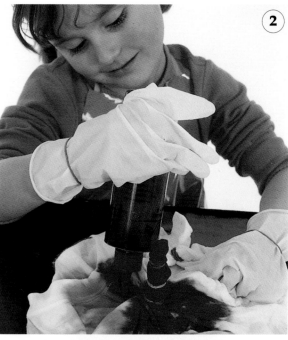

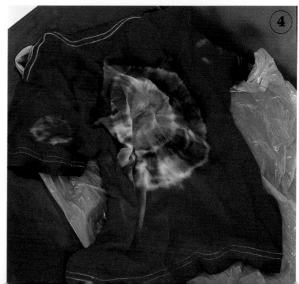

variation

• Try experimenting to achieve different effects. Tie off smaller and larger sections of fabric and see what effects you get from securing small buttons or stones with elastic bands.

tips

★ If you can't find a tie-dye kit, use cold-water dyes with a fixative. Paint the mixed dyes on with a brush or squirt them on using plastic bottles and following the instructions in the dye pack.

★ If you want to tie-dye several pieces in the same colour, dye them in the washing machine using a machine-wash dye.

peg doll

ages 4–6 years

A selection of national dolls made out of pegs shows how original and different costumes from other countries can look, using only a few scraps of lace, wool and ribbon. A monk's simple habit made from felt and string is a great contrast to an exotic Indian outfit made from bright ribbons. These festive dolls are entertaining and educational for all ages.

1 Paint a wooden peg all over with dark brown poster paint.

2 Tie a brown pipe cleaner around the peg below the face to make arms. Trim to the right length. Paint a simple face onto the front of the peg: two blue dots for eyes and a red dot for a nose and a mouth.

3 Glue one end of a green ribbon to the peg and wrap it around the body sari-style, leaving the arms protruding on either side. Glue the other end at the back and attach a gold sash or small tassel, if you wish. Glue a tiny roll of brightly coloured ribbon to the head as a turban.

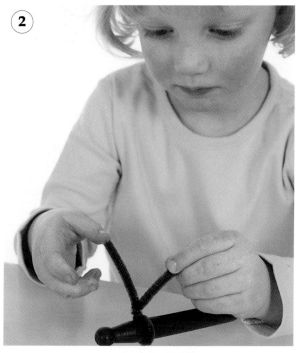

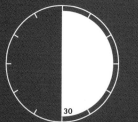

**time needed
30 minutes**

what you need

Old-fashioned
  wooden peg

Poster paint
  (brown, blue and red)

Brush

Brown pipe cleaner

Scissors

Glue

Coloured ribbons

variations

• Make an oriental doll using patterned paper or ribbon and black wool hair cut in a bob. Make a plait of wool for an Indian doll's hair and paint on a face with poster paint.

• Find out about festivals around the world and make dolls to represent the people of those countries. See how many different dolls you can make.

folding crocodile

ages 2–6 years

Folding decorations on sticks are fun for all ages to make. They are simply strips of paper made into creatures, insects or shapes, coloured in with crayons or felt-tipped pens and attached to wooden sticks. Adding ribbons makes them look especially festive. Pop them into a container as a decoration, play with them or use them to wave instead of a traditional flag at a festival.

1 Draw a rough outline of a crocodile: a long oblong with a pair of bulging eyes at one end and tapering tail at the other end. Make the top of the back a bold zigzag. Cut out the crocodile shape.

2 Draw in the eyes, mouth and nostril with a marker pen. Draw stripes down the length of the body and colour them in using different coloured felt-tipped pens.

3 Leaving the head and tail flat, fold the middle body section concertina-style.

4 Tape two wooden sticks to the wrong side of the crocodile, one near the front and one near the back.

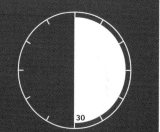

**time needed
30 minutes**

what you need
Paper
Pencil
Scissors
Marker pen
Felt-tipped pens
Wooden sticks
Sticky tape

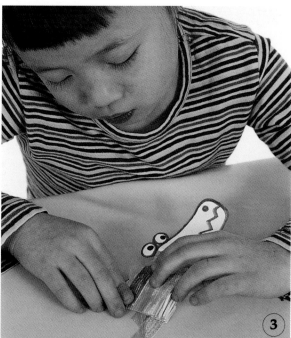

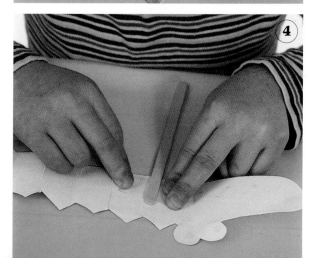

variations

mystical animals

Design your own creatures
and decorate them with glitter,
coloured spots or sequins.

paper fans

Fold and colour in an
elaborate fan, hanging ribbons
at the ends to jazz it up.

see-through crown

ages 2–6 years

This is surely among the best projects ever: it's very simple and quick to do, good fun for all ages, and the results are both stunning and satisfying. Using clear tape means there are endless ways of achieving a unique and imaginative festive idea.

time needed
10–20 minutes

what you need

Coloured or patterned paper

Scissors

Ruler

Glitter

Stars

Sequins

Very wide clear sticky tape

(1) Cut out narrow strips of coloured paper. Lay them in a line about 25 cm (10 in) long on a board or table. Sprinkle glitter, silver stars and sequins over the paper strips.

(2) Place one length of tape over your decorated band of coloured strips and press it down firmly. Carefully peel it off the table and turn it over. Press on another length of tape, so the paper and decorations are sealed in a pocket of tape.

(3) Make a second strip of paper and decorations in the same way and join the pieces of tape together with more tape to form a crown. Check your child's head size before you make the final join.

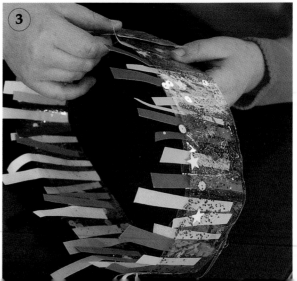

variations

spangly bangle

Use leftover pieces to make into a bangle. Pre-cut shapes, sequin strips and feathers are all suitable materials.

sticky ideas

Make a photo frame or a spotty dog brooch. Cut-up pieces of decorated tape can be threaded onto wire to make a necklace.

tips

★ It is easier to make two smaller pieces for a crown rather than one long one.

★ Turn the wide tape over to make a narrow decorative strip rather than using narrow tape.

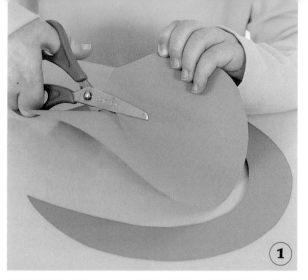

paper spiral decoration

ages 5–6 years

These festive paper hangings can be used indoors and out. The tissue paper flags look even prettier when there is a gentle breeze blowing. Inexpensive and quick to make, they can look simple or elaborate and, with parental help for very young children, a lot can be achieved in very short time!

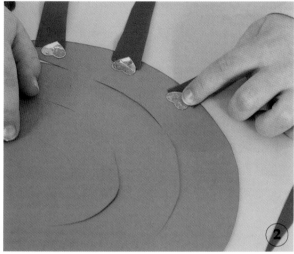

1 Use a plate to draw a circle on coloured paper. Cut it out. Draw a spiral shape inside the circle and cut it out.

2 Fold pieces of coloured tissue paper several times. Draw on and cut out several pointed flag-shapes. Attach these around the spiral using glitter stickers at even intervals.

3 Make a small hole at the top of decoration (the centre of the circle) with a pin and thread through a ribbon to hang it with. Knot to secure.

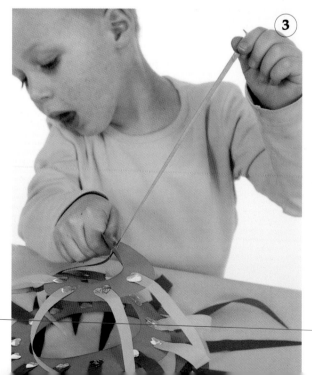

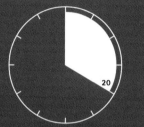

**time needed
20 minutes**

what you need
Plate
Coloured paper
Pencil
Scissors
Coloured tissue paper
Glitter stickers
Pin
Ribbon

variations

chinese lanterns

Fold a piece of paper in half lengthways. Make cuts at broad intervals along the fold, leaving the top and bottom edges uncut. Unfold the paper and tape the shorter ends together. Push into shape so it resembles a lantern and stick or staple on a handle.

tissue flags

Fold a piece of tissue paper into four and cut out different patterns. Unfold and glue top edge over a ribbon to make a hanging banner. Don't forget to use stick glue.

tips

★ Cut out several decorations at a time, for quick results.

★ Mix coloured foils and gold, silver and bronze tissue paper with plain colours for a sparkly finish.

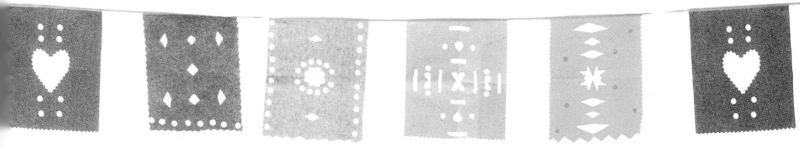

templates

On this and the following pages are all the templates required to make the projects in this book. All templates are shown at actual size. Percentage enlargement sizes are indicated where needed.

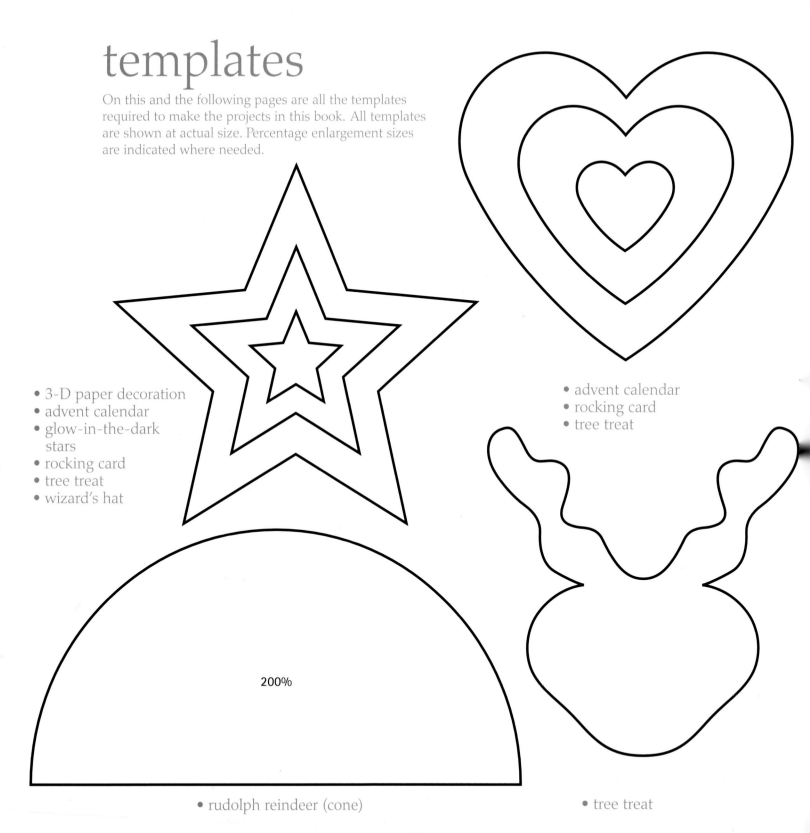

- 3-D paper decoration
- advent calendar
- glow-in-the-dark stars
- rocking card
- tree treat
- wizard's hat

- advent calendar
- rocking card
- tree treat

200%

• rudolph reindeer (cone)

• tree treat

200%

• Christmas stocking

• 3-D paper decoration
• advent calendar
• rocking card
• tree tree bag

• 3-D paper decoration

• apron card

• T-shirt card

• hat card

• bag card

200%

200%

200%

200%

200%

• shorts card

• butterfly gift tag

• loved-up T-shirt
• sweetheart photo
  frame
• valentine card

200%

• colourful flowers
• foam necklace

• flower photo frame

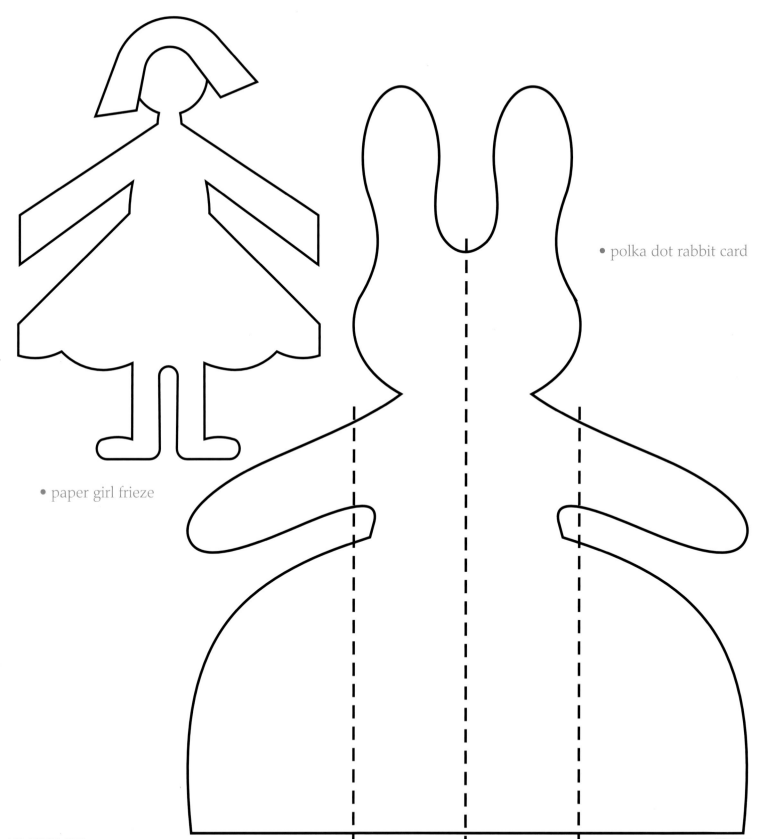

• polka dot rabbit card

• paper girl frieze

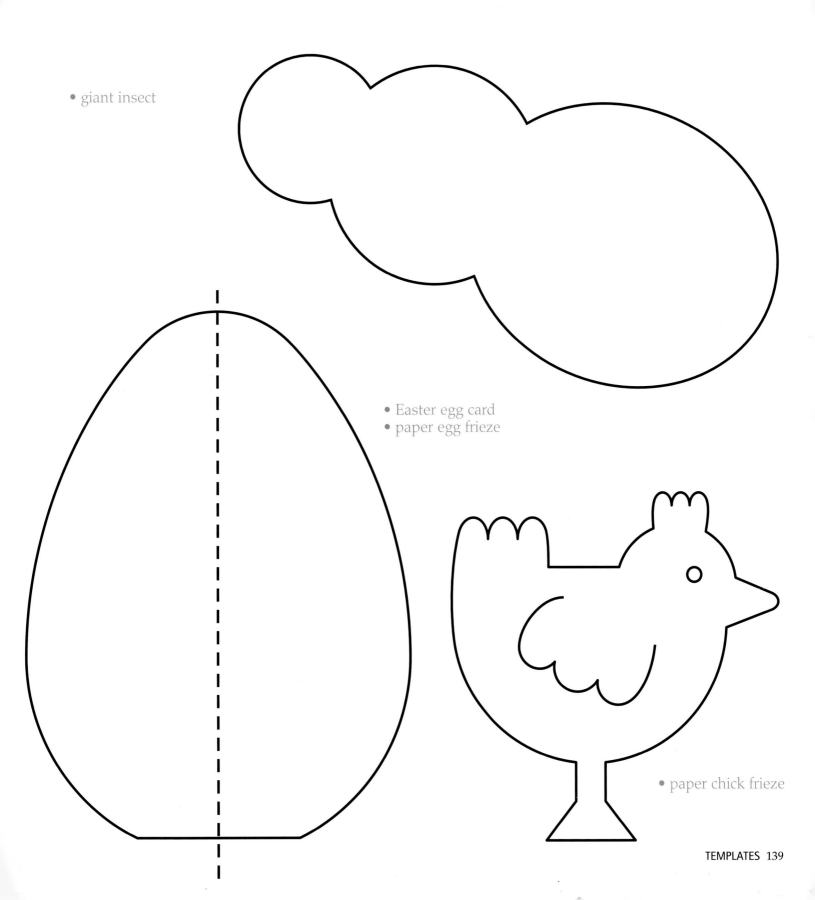

• giant insect

• Easter egg card
• paper egg frieze

• paper chick frieze

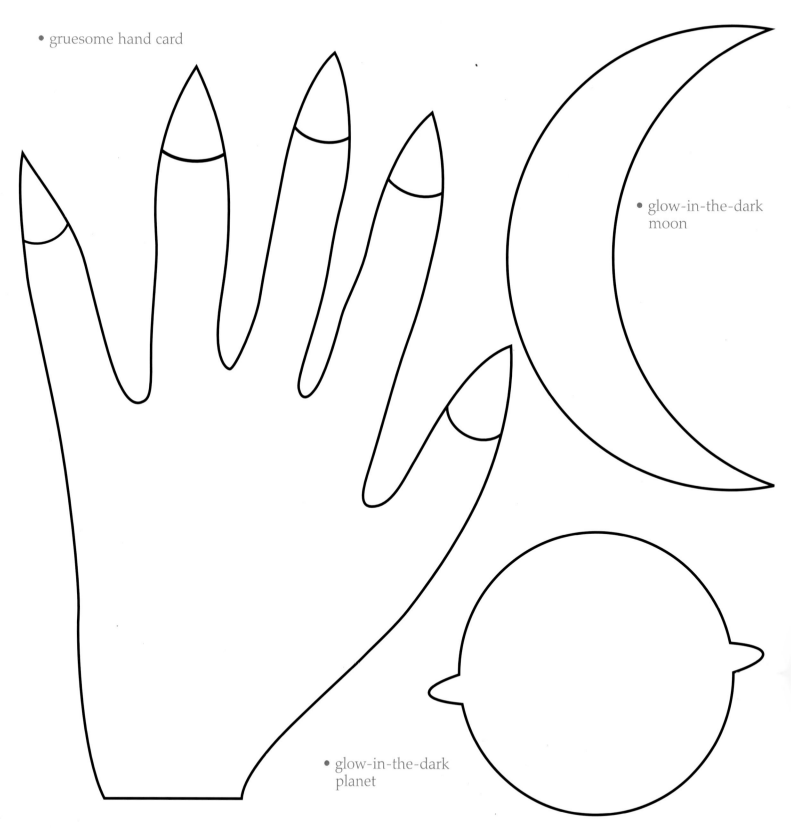

• gruesome hand card

• glow-in-the-dark moon

• glow-in-the-dark planet

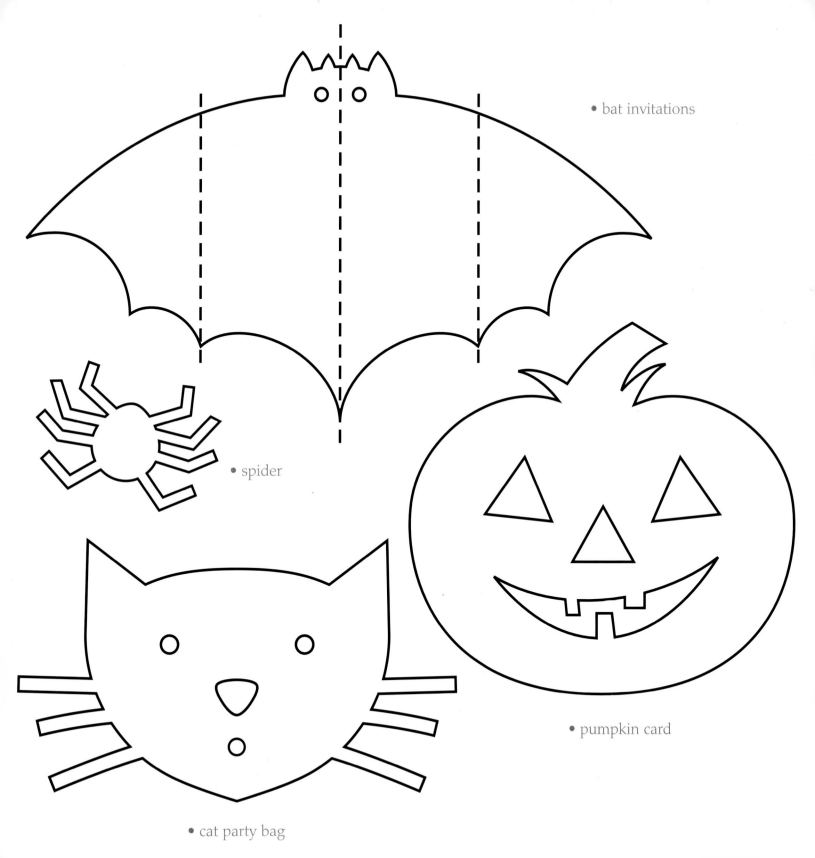

• bat invitations

• spider

• pumpkin card

• cat party bag

Index

Acknowledgements

The author and Publishers would like to thank Ben Avery, Luke and Neil Baldwin, Ellie Beed, Allie Bunyan, Leila Coleman, Sophie Davies, Ella-Dee, Jessamy and Mayes Fusco-Fagg, Joseph Gillan, Oscar Goldman, Nia Haugabrook-Evans, Charlotte and Daniel Leadley, Jake Mole, Eddie and Ella Roscoe, Alfi and Tobi Swain and Annie Weller for being such wonderful models.

Executive Editor Jane McIntosh
Managing Editor Clare Churly
Executive Art Editor Rozelle Bentheim
Designer Beverly Price
Production Controller Manjit Sihra
Special Photography Peter Pugh-Cook